Lenham and the Great War

Those who served in war and peace

Lenham and the Great War
Those who served in war and peace

Amy Myers

To Barry
Best wishes
Amy Myers

The Hatch Charity
Lenham

First published in 2014 by The Hatch Charity
Lenham Community Centre, 12 Groom Way,
Lenham, Kent ME17 2QT

ISBN 978-0-9928947-1-9

Printed in Britain by Lotus Design and Print Ltd. Rose Lane, Lenham Heath, Kent, ME17 2JR.

Contents

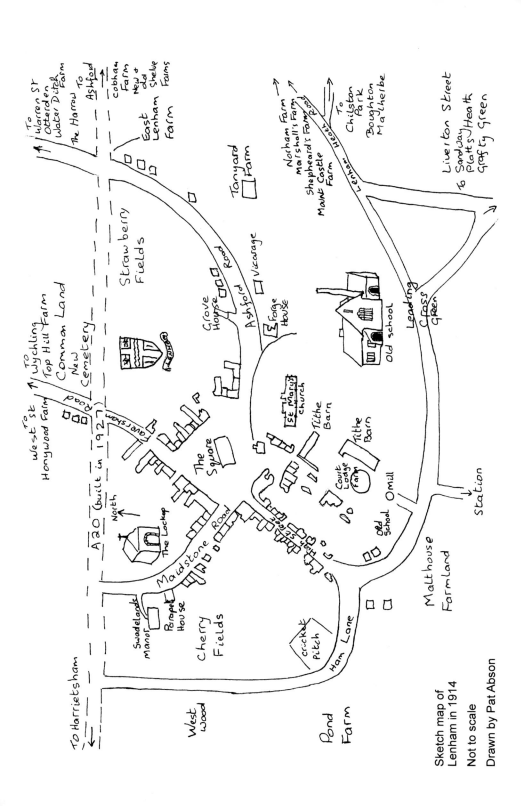

Sketch map of
Lenham in 1914

Not to scale

Drawn by Pat Abson

Introduction

James Troup Hatch and Nick Osborne, the present chair of the Hatch Charity, shared the same belief although they were separated by nearly a hundred years. They believed that the men from Lenham who served in the Great War of 1914-1918 should not be forgotten, whether they survived the war or were killed in action. Accordingly in 1920, when the Lenham memorial cross on the downs was in its planning stages, James Troup Hatch masterminded with the help of the village a list of the names and regiments of those known to have served in the war. He then pinned the resulting list in the porch of St Mary's Church in order that amendments and additions could be made.

Ninety-three years later Nick Osborne discovered the list, its pinhole still visible, buried at the bottom of a trunkful of papers relating to the charity that James Troup Hatch had set up in 1913. Nick too believed that these 258 men, together with two added afterwards, should be remembered in permanent form and that a book should chronicle their service to the country and to the village, not only during the war years but afterwards as well. From that list, 42 were killed in action. The majority returned to Lenham, coped with the ordeal of readjustment that was necessary, whether physical or mental, and once more became an integral part of Lenham's life.

These men were not the only people from Lenham to serve during the war; everyone faced a challenge. Farmers struggled not only to increase output but to do so with many of their former employees away at the front; the women, the children, the men counted unfit or overage for military service, and the elderly were by the end of the war all playing their part in Britain's survival in ways that would have been inconceivable before the war began.

One of the men deemed too old for active service was James Troup Hatch who was 58 in 1914. He had retired from farming at Old Shelve Farm and was living in Grove House with his wife Edith. He was one of thousands all over the country who helped establish unofficial volunteer battalions, which initially were frowned on by the government, eager to push its official recruitment drive, but as the months passed they were conditionally accepted.

Kent's commandant was the distinguished Lord Harris, known not only for his political career but his prowess in cricket. He organised the many volunteer groups into three regiments, East, Mid and West Kent, and James Troup Hatch became a lieutenant in the 5th Battalion West Kent Regiment. Later in the war the battalions were reorganised with closer affiliation to the regular county regiments, although James Hatch had to resign his commission in December 1917 because of ill health. The Volunteers were no Dad's Army. They played an active role in defence, and later in the war some went overseas. James Hatch, who in 1913 had established the Hatch charity, lived on in Lenham until 1933, Edith having died in 1926.

By that time the men on the list he had compiled were part of the backbone of Lenham, contributing on all fronts, employers, workers, football and cricket players and active in the church. Everyone knew them. Some were no longer able bodied, some seemed 'odd' to those who had never known them as active young men. Now very few Lenham people can remember them, and they knew them as 'old men' because they themselves were then children. Personal memories of those on the Hatch list are therefore sparse, but they live on in family traditions, in letters and journals and in photographs from which young hopeful faces gaze at us over the hundred year gap.

Letters quoted in the text are in their original form. For a community of mainly agricultural labourers and limited schooling, writing and spelling were hard, which makes their letters an even greater testament to how much soldiers at the front were missing home. The vast majority would not have left Kent before, let alone the country. Their military service and census records provide a basic skeleton for the majority of the men in the list. Unfortunately, for the First World War both present many problems. The major stumbling block for the former is the fact that over two-thirds of the service records for soldiers were burnt in a fire in the Second World War. Many of those that remain are partially burnt, providing tantalising gaps. Other records are more complete, but rarely give the soldier's home and birth details whereas a service record if available can provide not only these but the date of enlistment. Add to that human error in transcription of both service and census records, plus the variations of spellings, and the building of a complete picture of any one of the men on the Hatch list was seldom possible without their families' help.

It is a sobering task to look through the casualty and regimental lists and see the sheer number of men with identical names, which makes it hard to determine which one applies to Lenham. Many of the men on the Hatch list have little information recorded about them, and some of their names were not recognised even to those who grew up in the village before the Second World War. That suggests families either moved away after the war, or that the men's inclusion on the list was because they were temporarily working in the village or were relatives of those living in the village, such as sons who had moved away for work or marriage. The fact therefore that some men in the following pages are given more space than others only reflects the amount of information available about them, *not* the value of their contribution.

Of the names on the Lenham war memorial stone, several have proved untraceable, not just for this book but to other researchers, a fact that is reflected on many internet sites. Sometimes it is possible to disentangle the truth, sometimes to suggest a probability, or in one or two cases alternatives. Some who were killed in action from Lenham are not on its war memorial, perhaps because they died of wounds some years after their return, or perhaps because though living in the parish the families worshipped elsewhere and never saw the list, or in one case because of duplication of names.

In the pages that follow the choice of which men should be covered in each chapter is necessarily arbitrary, because of the lack of information, though I have done my best to work it out from what is available. There were some mistakes in the Hatch list over the regiments and names of some of the men, and there are bound to be a few incomplete or wrong assumptions in this book too, due to lack of information and the time lapse.

More men are included here than are on the Hatch list. Several are either buried or commemorated in Lenham cemetery, some have emerged from the shadows during the research for this book and others have close Lenham connections. The population in 1911 of the civil parish of Lenham was 1780 and that of the ecclesiastical parish was 1475, although the Hatch list does not pay strict attention to the parish boundaries. In any case these have altered in the last hundred years, as has Lenham itself. The A20 bypass of the village wasn't even a twinkle in the roadplanners' eyes – it came in 1927. The present Faversham road stretched right up to the downs, all traffic came through the village and much of the present housing was then open fields.

The chapter titles in this book are from the poems of Edward Thomas and appropriate as he lived for some years in Bearsted; his poetry was a belated outpouring of passion for the English countryside seen through the tragedy of war, and he died, as did many Lenham men, in the Battle of Arras in 1917.

This book was the result of James Hatch and the Hatch Charity's resolve, but it would not have been possible to write it without the firm support and enthusiasm of the descendants of the Hatch list men and other members of the village of Lenham; they are recorded with much gratitude in Chapter Seven.

My thanks are also due in particular to Nick Osborne and the trustees of

James Troup Hatch outside Grove House with the 5th Kent Volunteer Regiment

the Hatch Charity; to Mike Cockett for his magical mastery of the photographs; Steve Finnis, volunteer at the Queen's Own Royal West Kent Regiment Museum in Maidstone and to Christopher Jupp, the Regiment's archivist and historian, both of whom have provided their expertise and valuable information. I am also grateful to my husband Jim for his strong support, Hazel Basford, chairwoman of the Kent (East) Western Front Association, to Lesley Bellew and the *Kent Messenger,* to Pat Abson for her splendid work on the map of Lenham, to the Lenham *Focus,* to Kate Stansfield, Kinn McIntosh, Margo McFarlane, Jan Smith, Doris Frost, and Guy Lister, to the aviation authors Norman Franks and Alex Revell and to Marley Eternit for their much appreciated help. Also my thanks to Trevor Weekes and John Collins, the Revd Canon E.V. Binks, Pauline Appleton, Ian Durham and to Sarah Pearson and the Charing and District Local History Society team. Another team has been crucial in ensuring this book sees the light of day, Joan and John Perseval, from Lotus Design and Print in Lenham Heath, to whom my grateful thanks for their expertise and enthusiasm.

James Troup Hatch had no children, and on his gravestone in Lenham Cemetery are carved the words 'The Last of his Race'. He was a great benefactor to this village, and it is hoped that this book may also be as much a commemoration to him as it is to all the men who appeared on the list that he so painstakingly compiled.

One

Into the Unknown

From 'Lights out' by Edward Thomas

Tuesday, 4th August 1914. At Andrew Barr's East Lenham farm corn harvesting is underway, as at the many other farms in and around the parish of Lenham; the harvest is on the early side this year owing to the unusually hot summer. Yesterday was Bank Holiday Monday, and Arthur 'Pop' Hambley, the signalman at Lenham's railway station, has reported that the trains were packed not only with the usual holidaymakers heading for the seaside, undeterred by the political situation, but with naval reservists and foreign nationals rushing to return to their homelands. From the other direction flocked the British residents and holidaymakers who had struggled to catch the last trains and ferries back across the Channel to safety.

In the centre of Lenham all seems normal. Alfred Brown, the dairy farmer at Pond Farm, is making his twice daily delivery rounds with his sixteen-year-old son Edward. In The Limes, James Hughes is serving a customer in his greengrocery store and across Lenham Square his son John is inundated with telegraphs in his corner post office where the old Hussar alehouse used to be. George Chambers is serving stout and ale in the Red Lion pub, just as he has done for many years, and of his large family his three sons, Charles, Norton and Norman, are out and about working with the family wood business while his daughter Kate is helping him behind the bar.

Further along The Limes, a horse – perhaps Major Mitchell's from Swadelands Manor – waits patiently in the shade chained to one of the huge lime trees, while its owner chews over the grave situation with the saddler Alfred Palmer. At the far end of The Limes, the widowed coal merchant Mrs Tanton is talking earnestly to chimney sweep John Uden. Frederick Ellis is behind the bar in the Dog and Bear with his 21-year-old son Harold, and in the Faversham Road laundress Ellen Viner is dealing with the day's intake of sheets and towels. In his barber's and hairdressing room in Sunnyside, the family home behind the Red Lion in the Maidstone Road, Thomas Woolley is listening to his clients' views on Britain's future. Sarah, wife of Tom Gilbert, who works with horses and cows on a local farm, is greeting the Reverend Francis McDonald Etherington on the doorstep of her Church Square home. Two days ago, the vicar had led prayers for peace in St Mary's church, in response to the Archbishop's orders to churches all over the country.

In Lenham Heath, carrier George Chapman is delivering goods to postmaster cum shopkeeper William Bayley. In Grafty Green William Bellingham's post office is buzzing with customers, as is Frederick Sitford's at Sandway. At Otterden, Warren Street and Wychling, farmers are busy with the harvest as are George Fisher at Honywood Farm, helped by his son Edward, and Harry Clifford at Waterditch. It's not only harvest but fruit-picking time and all hands, young and old, are hard at work.

Everything *looks* normal enough, save that John Hughes hasn't had to break off his work for the usual routine of being called outside to greet Lord Chilston, who regularly arrives in his carriage from Chilston Park. Today Lord Chilston, former Home Secretary, is at Westminster where Parliament is battling with the current crisis.

It seems to have blown up from nowhere. Until three days ago, the most pressing problem being debated in Lenham's pubs, shops and homes was the gun-running and threat of civil war in Ireland. The assassination of the Archduke Franz Ferdinand on 28th June in Sarajevo by a Bosnian Serb and its effects on the Austro-Hungarian Empire and Germany were interesting, but have not directly affected Lenham or the cricket season which is going well for Kent or the holiday season which has just begun. So how has the situation changed so quickly that the Navy has had to be mobilised and it seems that Britain might be drawn into a European war?

On Lammas Day, Saturday 1st August, once the day when the first new corn was placed on the church altar, the news was that Austria's ally Germany had declared war on Serbia's ally Russia. As a result Russia's ally France mobilised the next day as German troops began to move towards Belgium, which everyone knows is a neutral country. Its ruler, King Albert, refused to allow Kaiser Wilhelm's troops to march through his country in order to attack France, with the result that Germany declared war on France and yesterday, Bank Holiday Monday, had entered Luxembourg and is now threatening to invade Belgium.

The British government has had to decide between the prospect of joining the war and the nightmare of the Kaiser engulfing the whole of Continental Europe up to the French coast. And as with the threat from Napoleon only a hundred years ago – and many people in Lenham remember hearing their parents and grandparents talk of invasion fears – the Kaiser would then cast greedy eyes on

England. Yesterday the Government made its decision and had sent an ultimatum to Germany to halt its plan for the invasion of Belgium within 24 hours.

The 24 hours will be up at 11 o'clock this evening, and Lenham, as is the whole country, is waiting. Some people still believe all this is mere sabre rattling by the Kaiser. After all, he is King George V's cousin, Queen Victoria's grandson and a great lover of all things English – especially the Cowes Regatta. Others believe the Kaiser should be taught a lesson, once and for all. He's tried this kind of bluff before. He needs a short sharp shock, a task that the regular British Army and Navy will make short work of. Some are more cautious, especially the women. Everyone in Lenham has seen the telegraphed mobilisation order for naval personnel outside the post office and railway station on Sunday, and the news is that in towns and cities food prices are already rising, as the country depends on imported food. In an agricultural village such as Lenham, however, at least food might be no problem. True the banks remain closed as a precaution, but again in a village that inconvenience can be dealt with.

By the evening, as eleven o'clock approaches, the expiry of the 24 hour ultimatum, the news has spread that the Germans have now invaded Belgium. Crowds are massing outside Buckingham Palace singing Boer War songs and 'Goodbye Dolly Gray' as they wait in excitement for the King to appear on the balcony, as confirmation that their country is now at war. Now that the die is cast and there are no more doubts either within the Government or in the country as a whole, a surge of spontaneous patriotism sweeps its way through the crowds, as the National Anthem is sung. As a young Londoner in the crowd, Norman Gladden, later wrote: 'There seemed small reason for misgiving at the time. Were we not shielded by the vastest and most powerful navy that the world had ever seen? And did not the spirit of Nelson still guide and guard our national destiny?'

In Lenham, John Hughes is still at work, and his wife Mabel takes the morse telegraph that Britain is at war with Germany. By the next day, it seems the whole world is joining in this war. The Austro-Hungarian Empire, the Russian, the French, the German – and the British. The invincible British Empire. Now it's happened. No doubts now. The Kaiser must be taught a lesson once and for all if our homeland and loved ones are to be safe.

Some Lenham residents were already at their action posts. Charles Bryant was aboard the battleship HMS *Formidable* as its chief cook. He had been born in Sussex where he met his wife Rosalie whom he married in 1905. By that time Charles was already a cook's mate in the Royal Navy, so at first, as he was based at Chatham, Rosalie lived with her sister in Lime Kiln Cottages in Lenham. When war was declared, however, he and Rosalie had their own Lenham home, Fairview.

Britain's Navy was still the envy of the world, and *Formidable* was currently part of the 5th Battle Squadron defending the Channel. Its first task was to provide cover for the transport of the British Expeditionary Force when it set off for France. The first troops sailed on 12th August, guarded by battleships.

Britain prided itself on its professional army, which was highly trained and skilled, and based entirely on volunteers rather than the alien conscription. Even the Territorials, set up in 1908 from the former militia, were somewhat suspect. The regular army was a small one, 'contemptibly' so, in the Kaiser's view, consisting of six divisions. The initial plan was to send four to France and keep the remaining two here for home defence. Its Navy however, still seemed Britain's strongest card.

George Hodgkin and his brother Lewis were much further away from Lenham than Charles Bryant when war was declared. He and Lewis were the

Lewis Hodgkin before the war

sons of widower George Hodgkin, who lived in Corks Court in Platts Heath with their sister Kate. George senior had not only had to endure the loss of his wife but of their oldest son Tom, who had died during service in India in 1898. Another son had been lost at birth, and both his remaining sons were on regular service far away.

On 4th August 27-year-old George junior was in Sydney, Australia. George had enlisted at Chatham for the Navy in 1903, at first on the training ship HMS *Lion* and then training for submarine work. Submarines were to play an increasingly important role as the war progressed and food supplies became crucial. In August 1914 George was currently on loan to the Australian Navy, and serving in submarine AE1. She and her sister

George Hodgkin with their sister Kate. 'I shall be glad when we all get together again,' wrote his brother Lewis on 27th October 1914.

submarine AE2 had been built in Barrow in Furness and commissioned into the Royal Australian Navy in February 1914; AE1 was manned by Royal Navy officers and a mixed crew of Royal Navy and Australian personnel. AE1's voyage out to Australia during the summer of 1914 had involved – hardly surprisingly – several breakdowns during which she had to be taken in tow by their Royal Navy escort. George described part of the voyage as 'a rolling trip in the Bay of Biscay'.

George's brother Lewis, five years younger than George, had enlisted in 1912 for the regular army, and was currently serving with the 2nd Battalion,

Lewis Hodgkin in uniform. 'It seems a little like home when we can get a paper to look at on a Sunday afternoon.'

Queen's Own (Royal West Kent Regiment) in Multan, India. Writing home from Dalhousie in August, where he had been stationed at least since April, he described his work as 'knitting in the hills' while they waited for action. It was to come soon enough. The battalion was part of 12th Indian Brigade. The Indian Government supported the war, and Indian troops were to serve on the Western Front, the Dardanelles, the Middle East and Africa.

By October Lewis had moved to Amritsar, and was writing home, '…we have had orders to move. We don't know where we are going… If we are bound for the front, I will write as often as possible…'

Farm labourer Harry Giles was also a regular and in the Queen's Own Royal West Kent Regiment. He had first enlisted in 1905,

George Hodgkin *(back row, second from the right)* with shipmates in Malta in 1906, celebrating their firing prowess

10

and joined the 1st Battalion. After serving in Malta and more recently in Dublin, he had gone into the Reserves, complete with a certificate for sobriety! He was recalled to the colours on 26th August. He had been born in Stalisfield in 1887, but his mother and siblings were living at Waterditch Farm at Warren Street by 1914. Lenham was Harry's base too, because a year earlier he had married Emma Jane from Ospringe and they now had a baby daughter Emily Violet. In 1911 when Harry had been living in barracks at Aldershot he had declared his occupation as musician. Whether this meant he was in an army band or that it was a civilian calling is unknown, but perhaps he was at least able to entertain his fellow soldiers on their time away from the front line.

Born in 1881, Fred Record, the youngest of the six children of Kate and Charles Record was living in Vine Cottages in Lenham High Street with his wife Mary. He, like Harry Giles, had also had plenty of experience in war, having served in the 2nd Boer War in South Africa early in the century with the 2nd Battalion The Buffs (East Kent Regiment). He had been a bricklayer when he enlisted in July 1900, and was in the Reserves in October 1912. Recalled, probably to the 1st Battalion, he reached St Nazaire in France on 10th September.

Like Fred Record, Charles Bugden, the son of William and Mary Bugden and born in Ulcombe in 1884, was a Boer War veteran and in 1914 was a Special

Fred Record's son Fred outside Lurcocks grocery store where he worked for his entire career save for six years serving in the Northamptonshire Regiment in World War Two

Fred Record *(standing far right)* at a Buffs' reunion in the 1950s

Fred Record's parents, Charles and Kate *(from a damaged photograph)*

Reservist, having en-listed for six years. The Special Reserve had been created, as had the Territorials, in 1908, as an addition to the regular army reserve. It differed from the Territorial Force in that men could be sent overseas, whereas the Territorials had a choice of whether to go or not. After war broke out, the Special Reserve was mo-bilised for full time ser-vice. Charles had signed up for the militia in 1899, and then served with the 3rd East Kent Regiment until discharged after the Boer War in 1902. By 1911 he was living in Barming with his wife Bessie and daughter Beatrice Mary and was employed as an engine driver, probably for farmwork. As a Special Reservist he was called up to join the Royal West Kent Regiment, probably the 1st Battalion, which left for France on 15th August.

On the farms in Lenham parish, it was all hands to the harvest and fruit picking which had to continue, despite the fact that some at least of their labouring force had either been recalled or volunteered for the forces. Some of their employees had been part time Territorials which provided very basic training on a part time basis for them which could be done with their local mates – the same idea as for the Pals Battalions further north. After the war broke out, it was still possible to enlist in the Territorials, but service was now full time, and from September onwards their right not to serve overseas was removed.

One of the local Territorials was Arthur James Clark. Early in the twentieth century a standing jest in Lenham was that if you walked down the street and met someone you didn't instantly recognise you'd have a fifty per cent chance of being right if you greeted him, 'Good morning, Mr Clark, or Good morning, Mr Smith.' There were certainly a lot of both Clarks and Smiths living in Lenham when the war broke out in 1914. The Clarks came from several different families, the best known being that of Samuel and Maria Clark who lived in Church Square. Samuel Clark was a builder and a big employer in Lenham at the time. His workshed was behind the Clark home where the former doctor's surgery used to be and which is now private housing. Sam and Maria's sons served during the war (see Chapter 3).

Arthur James Clark came from a different family. He and his brothers Ernest, Alfred and William were the sons of Charles and Annie, living, like Fred Record, in Lenham High Street. Charles was a bricklayer, but 26-year-old Arthur was an assistant postman. Arthur had spent four years as a Territorial in the Kent Cyclist Battalion. Cyclist battalions had existed since the 1880s, charged with communication in the defence of the coastline in the event of invasion, and in 1908 they became part of the Territorial organisation. On the outbreak of war, the Kent Cyclist battalion was mobilised and centred in Canterbury with duties involving the protection of the Kent and Sussex coast, but its role changed as the war progressed. Heavy army bicycles did not fare well over the rough terrain in northern France, and the men gradually became used as general infantry. The 1st Cyclist Battalion was sent overseas to India where it had many casualties. A memorial plaque can be seen in Canterbury Cathedral. Arthur James Clark, however, attested on 1st September, and joined the 8th Battalion Royal West Kent Regiment, which moved to France a year later, landing at Boulogne at the end of August.

His brother Alfred was five years younger than Arthur. A grocer's assistant, perhaps at Lurcocks in Lenham Square, he served as a lance corporal with the 2nd Battalion, Suffolk Regiment during the war. This was stationed in Khartoum when war broke out, but by the time Alfred Clark had done his basic training, it would have been in France, where it remained throughout the war.

Ernest John Clark was older than Alfred, but only a year separated him from Arthur. By 1911 Ernest was 26, married to Annie Harriet, living in Harrietsham and working as a master bricklayer. By the time he enlisted and joined the 10th Battalion, Devonshire Regiment, he had moved to Valana Cottages in Lenham Heath.

The eldest of the four brothers was William, who was 27 when war broke out. As will be seen from Chapter 2, however, there were two Williams on the Hatch list but it is probable that this William served in the Royal Army Medical Corps.

Edward Kemp was also a Kent Cyclist, living at Factory Cottages. He had been working as an engineer for Clark Maylam; he owned a farm machinery business in Lenham, which contracted threshing machines and ploughs out to local farmers including Andrew Barr at East Lenham. Edward was 28, and like Arthur had signed up for an initial four years in 1910.

He wasn't the only one to leave Clark Maylam during the war. Clark's sons Herbert and Stewart also served, and Herbert was also in the Kent Cyclists on coastal defence. It's not known if Stewart was too; probably not as he was three years younger. Herbert was 28 in 1914 and the family had come from Westwell. By 1911 however Herbert was living in Lenham Square and working in the family business. Stewart (spelling varies with Stuart in records) served as a corporal in the Royal Engineers during the war. The recruitment offices were usually good at using local talent where it would best help the war effort.

Another Kent Cyclist was Walter John Foreman (later known as John), who attested in December 1916 when he was 25 having earlier served as a Kent Cyclist for four years. He stayed with the Kent Cyclists during the war. Walter John worked devotedly at Chilston Park as a gardener.

The new secretary of War, Field Marshal Lord Kitchener, who took office on 6th August had very definite ideas on what might lie ahead and planned accordingly. Knowing that the regular army was too small to carry Britain through the long war that he expected (no 'over by Christmas' for him!) he planned for an army of 70 divisions, instead of the existing six. New armies would be required, and speedily if the soldiers were to be properly trained. If Kitchener had anything to do with it, they would be. He did not believe that the Territorial system could raise enough men; the situation demanded a whole bold new approach, and he took it.

Only a day later, he made his call for 100,000 volunteers aged between 19 and 30 for his New Army and the country responded with fervour. Recruiting offices sprang up, makeshift training centres covered England, his idea of pals joining the same regiment hit the right note, and men enlisted with eagerness. Even the veiled news of the disasters at Mons and Le Cateau did not deter men from recruitment, although by the end of August over 15,000 British men had been killed or wounded or were prisoners of war. Now Kitchener called for another 100,000 volunteers, despite the fact that training facilities and equipment were not yet up to the task of coping with the flood of volunteers. As yet, Kitchener was firmly against conscription, believing that volunteers would prove sufficient, as had for many centuries been the case.

The recruiting shows and songs at theatres and in the rudimentary cinemas, coupled in early September with Kitchener's famous recruiting poster, had their effect, and Lenham, as every other village and town, responded. Jacob

Morgan (always known as Jack) joined the Navy. Born in Stelling Minnis, he had settled in Lenham. He seems to have been under a lucky star in his Naval service. The first ship he joined in August at Chatham was the light cruiser HMS *Arethusa,* which had only recently been launched and hadn't yet had any sea trials. *Arethusa* was the flagship of the Commander of the North Sea Destroyer Force, and was in action almost immediately in a successful operation to cut off the retreat of German cruisers making for their home ports. *Arethusa* was badly damaged by shelling but with no loss of life, and she was back in action by Christmas Day. Thereafter she had a highly successful career until meeting her end in 1916 from a mine.

Most of Lenham's recruits joined the New Armies, however. Men like ploughman Harry Amon, who signed up on 1st September, just after the enlistment age was raised to 35. Harry was 35, and single. He joined the 6th Battalion Royal West

Jacob (Jack) Morgan, who served in the Navy in the First World War, seen here during his service in the Second World War as a special police constable

15

Kent Regiment, and after basic training went to France in June 1915. In the 1901 census he was working as a horseman and living at Old Shelve Farm with his parents. (Old Shelve was then run by William Bucknell, whose son Arthur also served in the war.) By 1911 Harry was living in the Red Houses in Ashford Road with his brother and still working with horses on a farm.

Thomas Gilbert from Church Square enlisted in the Royal West Kent Regiment in 1914, and it's probable he joined the 1st Battalion in 5th Division. He reached France on 26th January 1915. Later he transferred to the Labour Corps, set up in 1917 from the various regimental labour units. He and Sarah lived in Church Square with their daughter Ivy, who was fourteen. His occupation in 1911 was as a farm horseman and cowman, perhaps on the adjacent Court Lodge Farm.

William Glazier Swaffer signed up in October 1914 at age 28. A grocer's assistant, he was born in Charing, but had moved with his widowed mother Eliza to Lenham Heath where they were living in Rose Cottage. Perhaps he was work-

Ivy outside the post office where she worked   Thomas and Sarah Gilbert at Chilston Park

16

Thomas Gilbert with his wife Sarah and daughter Ivy in 1935

Thomas Gilbert at his garden gate in the 1930s. He was 'one of those people whom people just loved'.

ing for William Bayley, the sub-postmaster whose all purpose shop was open for a great many years. Eliza like Ellen Viner was a laundress, one of the few occupations women could take up in villages such as Lenham. The war would change that. William became a driver for the Royal Field Artillery.

The brothers Sidney *(left)* and Charles Reginald Obbard (always known by his second name)

Charles Reginald Obbard (always known as Reginald) was a farm labourer who had been born in Matfield. He attested on 8th September 1914 at the age of 18 or 19, by which time he was living at New Shelve Farm. He joined the 7th Battalion Royal West Kent Regiment, reaching France on 26th July 1915. His brother Sidney – there were eight children altogether – probably joined the forces later, as he was two years younger. He served as a lance corporal in the East Surrey Regiment.

Sergeant Reginald Obbard *(back row on the right)* in the Royal West Kent Regiment. His sergeant's boots look new - and so this photograph might be celebrating his promotion to acting sergeant on 15th February 1918

Archie Bates does not appear on the Hatch List or on the war memorial and yet he was Lenham born and is remembered in the cemetery on Armistice Day with a poppy, as are other casualties of both world wars. Archie was living in Lenham for the 1901 census, when he was six years old, but by 1911 he was living in Catford with his mother and his siblings (his father, C.J Bates, was not present on census day) and he was working as a clerk in a brewery. He attested on 1st September 1914, and gave as his preference of service the 3rd Hussars. His wish wasn't granted and he was assigned to the Duke of Cambridge's Own (Middlesex Regiment).

George Howe was 32 when he enlisted on 17th November 1914; he was a groom – perhaps at Swadelands Manor – and living in Grants Cottages, Lenham, with his wife Rosa and their three children. He served with the Army Service Corps. The Army tried to fit the job to the man if it could, so perhaps he was still working with horses during his army service.

Not far way from the Howe family, on the corner of Ham Lane, was Malthouse Farm, the land of which stretched over the area where the Robins estate now stands. This was the home of Donald G. Ambrose, the son of the farmer, Charles Ambrose. His elder brother Robert remained on the farm but Donald had developed a love for the sea. He was born in 1896, and, as his nephew, the current Don Ambrose, recalls, 'he was fun and a great entertainer'. He was about 19 when the war broke out and in the Merchant Navy. With much of Britain's food supply being imported, the merchant fleet had as many dangers to face in the Great War as in the Second World War.

'Need England fear?' This was Donald Ambrose's own caption written on the back of the photograph.

Donald Ambrose's nephew, the current Don Ambrose, as a small boy at the gate of Malthouse Farm on the corner of Ham Lane

Donald Ambrose's brother Robert, who later ran Malthouse Farm, with his pony after the war

Donald with his mother Annie enjoying an afternoon at the Shack, a building belonging to the corn and coal merchant L.J. Clark & Co. and situated where Mill Close now is.

The Boyd family
Back row: Thomas Boyd *(right)* and his brother Jimmy (James)
Middle row: Their parents, Robert and Margaret
Front row from the left: Thomas's sister Mary, brothers Robert and John and sister Margaret

As Lord Kitchener predicted, the war did not end at Christmas. Recruitment had slowed in the autumn, although men from Lenham were still volunteering. The records do not show when many of the Lenham men signed up, but the farms were increasingly missing the labour – Robert Boyd at New Shelve in particular, as one of his workers was his son Thomas. The Boyd family first came down as tenant farmers in the 1890s, although not initially to Lenham. Robert himself was born in Dover, and after taking tenant farms near Dover, in Rolvenden and in Kemsing, he bought his first farm in 1912 – New Shelve. Robert had six children in all, and invested in more local farms on their behalf. Thomas was 21 in 1914 when he volunteered and went to France on Christmas Day with the 12th County of London Regiment (the Rangers Battalion).

By the time Thomas Boyd reached France, a new form of warfare had begun after the First Battle of Ypres led to a stalemate, with both sides dug into a line of trenches that was to stretch from Switzerland to the sea, neither side having succeeded in outflanking the other before winter tightened its grip. Elsewhere, Britain had now declared war on Turkey, the first British landings in Mesopotamia had led to the British entering Basra, at sea the Battle of the Falkland Islands gave Britain a success, for which the German navy speedily took their revenge. In December four battlecruisers shelled Scarborough, Whitby and Hartlepool with several hundred casualties. War was being waged on the home front.

When war was declared and war fever was at its height, women had no official role assigned to them. The Suffragettes' pleas for women to be given war work were falling on deaf ears, so Lenham women as elsewhere acted independently. They obviously stepped in where they could to fill the gaps left by their menfolk. Many organisations sprang up, including Soldiers' Comforts Funds, Sailors' Comforts Funds, the Queen's Work for Women Fund and Suffragists' workshops. Shortly the Women's Volunteer Reserve, the Women's Auxiliary Force and the Women's Legion were formed.

However it was in nursing and other hospital work where women rushed to help the national effort. Young women such as Meg Woolley from Lenham threw themselves into training as VAD (Voluntary Aid Detachment) nurses, now that the numbers of wounded men returning to Blighty (as home was called), made the need for them evident. Lord Chilston was the county director for the British Red Cross and St John Ambulance, work for which he received the GBE after the war. He too had his family worries, as his son was in the Foreign Office working in Bucharest when war broke out.

One more factor affected Lenham in the early months of war, the Belgian refugees who had fled across the channel to Folkestone and Dover and needed emergency housing. The Village Institute was turned over to them, and women cooked for them and generally helped them until the Belgians were moved on by the authorities. At the end of the year, however, a new threat loomed over Lenham. The first Zeppelin had been seen in British skies.

What happened to the men from Lenham

Donald Ambrose survived the war and remained in the P & O Merchant Navy as an electrical engineer. His brother Robert ran Malthouse Farm after his father's death, and Robert's son still lives in Lenham, another Don. His mother, Robert's wife, was Kate Chambers from the Red Lion pub. Although the farm has disappeared under the Robins estate, the farmhouse is still on the corner of Ham Lane.

Tragically, after surviving the war, Donald G. Ambrose, 'the great entertainer', died of appendicitis about 1926 on board ship in the China Seas. He is buried in Shanghai.

Harry Amon became first a lance corporal and then a corporal in the 6th Royal West Kent Regiment, and in 1916 was transferred to the 250th Tunnelling Company which was responsible for the dangerous work of digging deep level tunnels for mines, including those for the massive explosions at Messines Ridge in 1917. In September 1917 Harry was awarded the Military Medal for his work, but the following year on 20th March he was wounded and returned to Blighty. He was sent to the Roehampton for treatment, the hospital that specialised in pros-thetic limbs, and, no longer physically fit for service, was discharged from the army in February 1919. He was granted a pension of 21s 8d a week (£1.09 today). Don Ambrose remembers Harry Amon well. He was still living with his brother in the Red Houses on the Ashford Road and 'he always walked lame', Don says.

Archie Bates: Lance Corporal Bates died in Salonika on 27th February 1917 and is buried in Salonika's military cemetery. Malaria was widespread on the Balkan front and whether his death was due to that or wounds is not known. Although his immediate family seems to have moved to London there were many Bateses living in and around Lenham then, some of them probably relatives who were responsible for the memorial to him in Lenham cemetery.

Thomas Boyd: Thomas survived the war and returned to New Shelve Farm. The farms that his father had bought were in due course shared among his six children to run. Thomas thereafter farmed at New Romney Farm, although in 1922 he was competing as a driver for his father in a Class 8 Farmers' Tractors competition held by the Ashford and District Agricultural Society at East Lenham Farm on 1st November. The task was to plough one and a half acres in five hours. Perhaps he won the extra prize of 15 shillings (75p) awarded for setting out and finishing!

Charles Bryant: By the end of 1914 Charles was at Portland, where *For-midable* was now based. New Year's Eve brought exceptionally rough weather, and no one was expecting German U-boats to be anywhere nearby. But they were. *Formidable* was off Start Point when early on New Year's Day she was torpedoed by *U-24*. Orders were given to abandon ship, but even the cruisers and lifeboats could not save all the crew, 547 of whom were lost. One of them was Lenham's Charles Bryant.

The loss of the *Formidable* was a heavy blow for the Navy, but it had one unexpected result. Many of the dead were laid out in the cellar of a Lyme Regis pub. The pub's owner had a collie dog, who lay down beside one of the men, licking his face and sharing its warmth with him. The man eventually responded and made a full recovery. The dog's name was Lassie – and it was the inspiration for the famous Lassie films.

After Charles's death his wife Rosalie remained in Lenham, and was a regular donor to St Mary's.

Charles Bugden joined the 1st/4th Leicestershire Regiment after the Royal West Kents, and was killed in France on 28th October 1918, aged 36, during the final advance in Picardy. He is buried in St Sever, and is on the Lenham memorial stone, although not on the Hatch list, probably because his family were in Ulcombe and did not hear about the list.

Alfred Clark survived the war, as did *Ernest* and *William.*

Arthur James Clark was invalided home from France after his service with the Kent Cyclists and the Royal West Kent Regiment, but attested again for future service on 26th March 1919.

Walter John Foreman (known later as John) survived the war and returned to Chilston Park as gardener, where he worked for very many years. His last words were said to be: 'What are they doing for slugs up there?'

Thomas Gilbert: Part of 5th division, the 1st Battalion Royal West Kent Regiment endured the Somme battles, then went to a quieter part of the line, then to Italy for five months, returning to France for the bitter fighting of 1918. Thomas returned safely to Sarah in Church Square, however, even though on at least one occasion it had been touch and go. He had been buried in mud at the Somme. 'It was only because somebody saw his eyelids flicker whilst he lay there that he was saved,' says his great-granddaughter Sarah.

After the war Tom Gilbert became one of Lenham's most popular and well known residents; he was a general carrier both of corn and other missions for the village and his horse and cart were a familiar sight. Anything wanted from the Maidstone shops and Tom would get it for you. He kept the horse and cart in what's now called Bank Yard, tucked behind the shops on the junction of Maidstone Road and the High Street. His daughter Ivy Lily Alice worked in a local post office (possibly Sandway) and later played for the village women's cricket team. Tom died in 1954 – with only one regret, as Sarah recalls: 'I remember my mother telling me how disappointed and angry he was about not being allowed to join up for World War II due to his age.'

Harry Giles: On 14th September 1914, shortly after he had reached France, Harry was wounded in the knee and on 24th June 1915 he was discharged as no longer fit for service. He was given a pension and returned to Lenham and his family. However he decided to settle in his wife's home village of Ospringe –

where, I hope, he could continue his musical career.

George and Lewis Hodgkin: In September 1914 AE1 was part of the Australian Naval and Military Expeditionary Force on a successful mission to capture German New Guinea. A day after the surrender of Rabaul, AE1 was lost with all hands including George Hodgkin, due it is thought to accident rather than enemy action. No trace has ever been found of her, although searches are still ongoing. George's last letter home was written on 13th September 1914, the day before he died. It read in part:

> I am sorry to say our landing party lost 2 officers and 4 seamen
> killed and 7 wounded in taking the wireless station on this island
> which is properly named New Briton. Our brigade was successful
> and we've captured a few small ships but can't find the German fleet
> yet. [Rabaul] surrendered today and we hoist the British flag at three
> this afternoon. … One poor fellow fell overboard yesterday from
> "The Australia" and was eaten up by sharks. …It's very hot up here
> and the place our fellows attacked was trenched and mined….
> With fond love, George.'

The Hodgkin family had another tragedy to endure when *Lewis Hodgkin* died on 24th August 1916. He had gone with the 2nd Royal West Kent Regiment, part of the 12th Indian Division to Basra, when the Mesopotamian Front opened up in early 1915. In October 1914 he had written to Kate:

> I was very sorry to hear the news about George. I had been
> wondering if he was on that submarine when I saw the account
> of the accident in the papers last month. I have kept looking for
> a list of the crew and it was in last week's paper I saw his name in
> the list of missing and I can guess how you feel about it at home.
> I'm sure it must have upset Father a good bit. I hope I'm spared to
> see the Dear Old Home again….It must have been an awful death
> being shut in one of those things.

When Lewis heard that they were going into action, he wrote: 'We don't know where we are going, it is a very quick move. We might be going to war for all we know....With fondest love to all, I remain your loving brother Lewis.' And scribbled underneath, 'Cheer up and don't worry too much.' She had need to. In another letter he jokes that he supposes all the nice girls would be married by the time he got back. Lewis wasn't destined to return to Corks Court, the home to which he longed to return. He had the misfortune to be in one of the two companies in the battalion that was besieged by the Turks in Kut-al-Amara and underwent terrible privations there – a fellow prisoner, John Sporle, described it as 'living like rats in the ground', as lack of food, constant shelling and sickness took their daily toll. On 29th April 1916 the garrison capitulated and its defenders were taken prisoner. Kate's letter to Lewis, full of news about Christmas and sent on 29th December 1915, was returned marked 'undelivered through capitulation at Kut'. Lewis died in captivity of dysentery in the appalling conditions of Turkish 'care'. He is buried in Baghdad.

George Howe: returned to Lenham safely and remained in Lenham. For unknown reasons, he was later known as 'Treacle' Howe – at a guess because of the local 'urban myth' of a treacle mine in the area.

Edward Kemp survived the war but his later life is unknown.

Herbert and Stewart Maylam: both survived and returned to the family business. The Kent Cyclists which Herbert had joined became an infantry battalion in 1916 and was sent to India, remaining there for the rest of the war. However it seems that Herbert must have transferred to the 1st/4th Royal West Kents which went to India in 1914. Both the Kent Cyclists and the 1st/4th RWK won the India General Service medal 1908-35 with clasp 'Afghanistan NWF' for the Third Afghan War.

The firm of Clark Maylam in due course became Clark Maylam & Sons. In 1913 Clark had advertised himself in *Kelly's Directory* as an agricultural machines owner and road roller and by 1918 he was concentrating on steam ploughs and road rollers. Clark Maylam was a trustee of the Hatch Charity but resigned in 1933. His sons Herbert and Stewart are remembered as being 'chalk and cheese' in abilities, so when Clark retired one ran the organisation and the other the practical side of the business. Their sister Norah became a VAD in Stanfield House (see Chapter Two) during the war and after the war opened a private school behind the present butcher's shop. That didn't stop her association with Stanfield House, however, as after the war the house reverted to being the doctor's home and surgery for which Miss Maylam dispensed prescriptions.

Jacob (Jack) Morgan remained in the Royal Navy for the duration of the war, and was again fortunate. From the *Arethusa,* he was sent to the armoured cruiser *Black Prince,* which had returned after an operation in the Red Sea (during which she captured two German liners) and an abortive mission off the African coast. She joined the Grand Fleet in December 1914. In 1916, *Black Prince* took part in the Battle of Jutland, and it was here that in disputed circumstances she was sunk with all hands. Over 850 men died.

For whatever reason Jacob Morgan was not serving on *Black Prince* at the time, and at the war's end returned safely to Lenham. He married his second wife, Ena Honeybun, in 1930, and lived in Hatch Row in the High Street, so named as James Troup Hatch owned the houses. It was familiarly known as Chatterbox Row, now demolished and rebuilt with newer houses. Jack became a special constable in the Second World War, and died in 1958. He had three children with Ena, one of whom remains a Lenham resident.

Kenneth Obbard during his service in World War Two. He was the youngest Obbard brother, born in 1915.

Reginald and Sidney Obbard: Reginald's battalion suffered heavily in the war both at the Somme in 1916 and on the first day of the German attack in 1918. He was by then an acting sergeant. Both he and Sidney returned safely to Lenham and the family home in Burnside Cottages near East Lenham Farm. Their brother Kenneth was too young to serve. The Obbard family still lives in the Lenham area.

Fred Record was discharged from reservist duties in 1919. He and Mary had six children, Fred, Margaret, Albert, Nellie, Alice and Kathleen, and the family is still in the Lenham area. His son Fred worked for many years in Lurcocks, the grocery in Lenham Square, and Fred himself worked postwar at steam ploughing for Clark Maylam, on contracts which sometimes involved sleeping in a farm hut for a week. He died in 1957.

William Swaffer died at home in 1918 aged 28. He had been discharged from the army through sickness, and a long fight has now been won to recognise him as one of the casualties of war. He lived in Lenham Heath, and appears on the Charing Heath memorial, since the two communities are close to one another.

Two

When the War's Over

From 'As the Team's Head-brass' by Edward Thomas

On the Western Front the new year of 1915 brought new strategies to end the war. Instead of ending it, however, March saw the battle of Neuve Chapelle and more heavy losses. The blame fell on the shortage of shells, and the outcry led to David Lloyd George becoming Minister of Munitions in May. The new year also saw the opening of a new front for Britain. Turkey, the central power of the old Ottoman Empire, 'the sick man of Europe' as it had been dubbed, seemed an easy target now that it had entered the war. Now that British and Indian troops had landed in the Ottoman province of Mesopotamia and taken Basra, they were preparing to advance further with Baghdad in their sights. But Winston Churchill's hopes of a successful quick naval attack on the narrows of the Dardanelles were dashed, and Kitchener's plans for a military assault to take the Gallipoli peninsula first were adopted rather than a second direct naval operation. In April therefore the Gallipoli landings commenced with British and Australian forces. Under their inspiring leader Mustafa Kemal, the Turkish troops were not the pushover that the British had expected, however. The bitter fighting continued until there was as much a stalemate there as on the Western Front.

There, also in April, the Second Battle of Ypres had begun, with the first introduction of gas as a weapon of war. War was escalating on the home front too. Following the shock of the bombardment from the sea in December, nightmare now struck from the skies as the dreaded Zeppelin attacks began. May brought a further horror that shook not only Britain but the United States which had remained neutral in the war. The passenger ship *Lusitania* was sunk with enormous loss of life, and brought the message that there were to be no exceptions in this new kind of warfare.

In 1915 Lenham, as elsewhere, began to get to grips with the fact that the war was here to stay much longer than anticipated and started to organise itself. The coal shortage was biting, as Mrs Tanton whose business depended on knew all too well, and there were rapidly rising food prices as Germany began to target merchant shipping. The farmers continued to lose their labourers, as with voluntary enlistment there was nothing to prevent their leaving the land if they wished. With farming dependent on horse and steam power, farmers faced difficulties caused by Army recruitment of horses and lack of workmen, spare parts and coal to use the steam ploughs. As yet, the Government was doing little to help the farmers' situation, but this would change during the year.

Dr John Temperley Grey, the commandant of VAD Detachment 134 hospital at Stanfield House and much appreciated GP for Lenham and Boughton Malherbe

Major changes were taken place elsewhere in Lenham too. The Belgian refugees had been moved on by now, but wounded soldiers were arriving in Kent in vast numbers. The Red Cross were establishing auxiliary hospitals to cope with them, and appealing for more. The popular Lenham doctor, Dr John Temperley Grey who lived with his wife Bertha, their son and three daughters in Stanfield House in Lenham Square, which was also his surgery, answered the call and offered the building as a hospital. He and his family moved out to a nearby cottage in order to provide more beds. Stanfield House could take 20 patients and it became part of VAD Detachment hospital No. 134, together with Harrietsham. The Foresters Hall, now the Lenham Social Club, offered a further 15 beds.

Voluntary Aid Detachments were first formed in 1909 to provide nursing services in the field and in hospitals, and as the war progressed they served overseas as well as in the UK. With the outbreak of war, young women flocked to train and join the service. Meg Woolley, daughter of Thomas Woolley, the hairdresser and barber at Sunnyside, had been a dressmaker before her VAD training, but now eagerly offered to work at Stanfield House as did Norah Maylam, the sister of Herbert and Stewart. In all

Meg Woolley, one of the VADs at Stanfield House and sister to Harry, Robert and Thomas. The photograph was taken by Herbert E. Birdsey, a well known St Albans photographer of the time.

VADs outside Stanfield House, Meg is on the right of the second row

seventeen staff were recruited. Dr Temperley Grey was the commandant and medical officer and a Miss Plowman the lady superintendent. The new hospital was officially opened on 15th May 1915 and the village rallied round to support the hospital in any way they could.

By the beginning of 1915 the first flood of volunteers for the New Armies had slowed, despite the urgent need for more men. Strongly opposed to conscription, Field Marshal Lord Kitchener still maintained that the volunteer system would meet the situation. Although men including many from Lenham volunteered as the year wore on, it became clear even to Kitchener that drastic measures had to be taken. As a gingerly taken step towards conscription, a national register was compiled in July to record the names of all able bodied people of both sexes from 15 to 65, and this, to the relief of farmers, 'starred' skilled workers, which meant that recruitment offices should discourage them from enlisting. This would include horsemen, waggoners, foremen etc.

The next step was the scheme instigated by Lord Derby, the Director General of Recruitment, whereby all men between the ages of 18 and 41 who were on the National Register should be asked to attest and they would be called up on the basis of single before married men and younger before older. 'Starred' workers were exempted. The scheme, introduced in late October 1915, failed to produce enough recruits and so the writing was on the wall. On 25th May 1916 able bodied men from 18 to 41 became subject to compulsory enlistment.

Many Lenham men had not waited for conscription, however, and volunteered during 1915. Farmworker George Edward Coppins had volunteered on 4th March at 19 years old. He was the son of Horace and Jane Coppins, and he was living and working at Great Pivington Farm. He joined the 6th Royal West Kent Regiment, and on 1st June the battalion crossed to Boulogne. Four other men from Lenham served in the war with the name of Coppins, but not, as far as is known, from the same family. One of them was also called George.

Twenty-four year old John Barton from Boughton Malherbe was the son of the carpenter and builder Richard and his first wife Louisa, and was working for his father. He enlisted on 11th January 1915. He asked to go into the Buffs, and his wish was granted. He served in the 2nd Battalion, which had recently returned to England from Madras. By the time he joined it on 9th June 1915, however, it was in France and part of 85th Brigade, 28th Division. His two brothers also served in the war. His twin brother Percy served as a sapper with the Royal Engineers and their older brother Frank, 29 and like John a carpenter, served in the Royal Army Ordnance Corps.

The Cox family also sent three sons to the war, Fred and his brothers Frank and Percy, who were all Lenham born. Fred was 22 years old and manager for the London Meat Company butcher's shop at the foot of Gabriels Hill in Maidstone, when he volunteered at the beginning of the war. He joined the 21st Lancers in Woolwich, but was transferred to the Rifle Brigade and sent to France in the summer of 1915. When Fred joined it in June, the 2nd Battle of Ypres was over, but fighting still continued in the Ypres area. Fred was pitchforked straight into battle on the Belgian front. Frank Cox was 20 in 1915, unmarried and working as a farm milkman. He served with the 9th Lancers. Percy served with the East Surreys later in the war – in 1915 he was only 16.

Another volunteer early in 1915 was Arthur Joy, who enlisted in February at age 26. He had been born in Maidstone but was now working and living at Swadelands Manor (now demolished and on the site of the present Swadelands Close) as a 'motor driver' – the fancy word 'chauffeur' wasn't yet in common use – for the Mitchell family. Arthur used his skills during his war service as a driver with the Army Service Corps (which added the Royal to its name late in 1918).

Gordon Mitchell, whose father Major Henry owned the manor, was 19 in 1915. His father, born in 1857, had been the surgeon major to the 2nd Life Guards, and had come from Yorkshire where he had owned another property. By the time of his marriage in 1895 and his son Gordon's birth they had settled in Swadelands Manor, an eighteenth century building set in a large estate, which is the site of the present Swadelands and Primary Schools, Mitchell Close, Swadelands Close and the Bowling Green. An army career was a natural for Gordon, who went to France on 28th July 1915 as a second lieutenant in the Royal Field Artillery.

Gordon Mitchell of Swadelands Manor in the Lenham cricket team in 1935 *(front row, third from left)*. Other players who appear on the Hatch list are: Sam Clark *(front row, second from left)*, Louis Clark *(fourth from left)* and the umpire Fred Clark.

Percy Oliver Merton (or Murton) was born near Folkestone in 1894 to Henry and Emily. By 1911, however, he was living and working in Smeeth as a farm waggoner. In 1915 he enlisted at Maidstone, by which time he was living in the Sittingbourne area. After his basic training he joined the 7th Battalion Royal West Kent Regiment which landed at Le Havre on 27th July 1915. His Lenham connection is not clear, but it is possible that at the time of his enlistment he was working on a farm that spanned land both in the Lenham parish and Frinsted, Sittingbourne.

The farm might have been Syndane (Sindane) Farm, owned by Charles Brakefield, whose son, also Charles, was 21 in 1915 when he attested on 11th December. He had been working for his father as a waggoner, now a starred category. Nevertheless he joined the Middlesex Regiment.

In July Frederick Ernest Fellows had volunteered at Maidstone at age 33. He declared his occupation as railway servant goods porter. He was born in Sussex and it might have been for that reason that, although living in Lenham in Mill House, he joined the Sussex Volunteers early in the war, which like the Kent

31

Volunteer battalions had sprung up in response to the crisis. He was married to Mabel Howe with three young daughters, Dolly, Olive and Ethel. When he had met Mabel, she had been a servant in Grove House, where James Troup Hatch lived, the founder of the Hatch Charity and during the war serving in the Kent volunteer forces. Mabel was the daughter of George Howe of Lenham (not the George Howe on the Hatch list), who lived in Maidstone Road. Having had some military experience with the Sussex Volunteers, Fred Fellows enlisted and joined the 10th Battalion of the Royal West Kent Regiment, which was raised in Maidstone in May 1915. A year later it went to France – shortly before the Somme offensive.

Laundress Ellen (Kit) Viner in Faversham Road, Lenham, saw both her sons, Earle and Arthur, leave for the war. Arthur was the elder of the two, at 25 in 1915. He was working at the L.J. Clark's corn and coal business, and joined the 7th Battalion, Royal West Kent Regiment, as had other Lenham men. Earle was two years younger than Arthur and had been living and working as a gardener at Chilston Park with Walter John Foreman, the Kent Cyclist. Earle reached France with the Worcestershire Regiment, probably with the 11th Battalion which crossed on 21st September after training in Wiltshire. It arrived only days before the Battle of Loos began, but it was not heavily involved in the battle, as it was sent to Fouilloy for more training, including in trench warfare. It would not be long, however, before the situation dramatically changed.

Frank Wickens

Frank Wickens, the son of Joseph and Annie, was living not far away from Chilston in Lynwood House, Boughton Malherbe, and was working on his father's farm with his brothers George and Robert until he volunteered at 21. He joined the 2nd/5th Buffs (East Kent Regiment), but was almost certainly in the company that formed part of the Kent Composite Battalion and also included companies from the Royal West Kent Regiment. On 20th July 1915 it left Southampton for the Gallipoli campaign, reaching Suvla Bay on 10th August, during fierce fighting there in yet another attempt to break the Turkish resistance so that naval passage could be forced through the Dardanelles.

Robert Wickens   Robert Wickens before the war

Frank's brother George also served with the Royal West Kent Regiment, at first with the 1st/1st Royal West Kent Yeomanry. He too served in Gallipoli, leaving England on 8th October. He was barely 18, if that. His brother Robert, a shoeing smith, was 19 when he enlisted under the Derby Scheme on 22nd November 1915. He joined the Army Service Corps where he pursued his career with the horses and mules as a farrier. The mules were bad-tempered and his daughter Marjorie remembers his saying they were 'always kicking out'.

James and Annie Wickens *(seated)*, uncle to Frank and Robert, at their home in Boughton Malherbe. The family members or friends have not been identified.

Charles Ottaway from Sandway was another volunteer. There is some doubt, but the records suggest that as did Frank Wickens he served in the composite battalion of both 2nd Buffs and two companies of the 2nd/4th Royal West Kent Regiment, and he appears on the RWK roll. He arrived in Gallipoli in August and the battalion later served in Egypt and Palestine.

Also serving in Gallipoli was Lieutenant Richard Eric Rutland Webster, who was first with the Royal Horse Artillery and later with the Royal Field Artillery. He too was in Gallipoli in November, but by the end of the month he was in Egypt after the evacuations from Gallipoli. His records suggest that he was living in Sandway, perhaps in Elmstone Lane, that he was born in 1886 and brought up in Richmond, Surrey.

Albert Wiffen and his brother Harry had also volunteered in 1915. They were the sons of George and Annie Wiffen, and living in Cygnet Cottages, Sandway, with them and their three sisters, Daisy, Frances and Dorothy. Their father George was a carpenter on an estate, probably Chilston Park, and Albert, then 19, was a general labourer, perhaps also on the estate. Harry was a carrier and 25 when he enlisted. Albert joined the 6th Battalion, Royal West Kent Regiment, and reached France on 1st June. In September the battalion was heavily involved in the Battle of Loos.

Daisy Wiffen, sister to Albert and Harry, standing on the left, and her sister Dorothy seated on the grass.

Daisy Wiffen *(seated)* in her days of service before the war

Albert's brother Harry, was 25 in 1915, chose a different path and became a sergeant in the Military Mounted Police. About 25,000 mounted police served in the war, most of them on the Western Front. Harry however served in Egypt. There was a small army force in Egypt when it became a protectorate in 1914, its role to guard the Suez Canal, then under British control, but when in late 1915 troops were evacuated from Gallipoli to Egypt, the force was greatly strengthened.

Harry Woolley (right) outside his Watford grocery store before the war with his brother Robert. The store's name predated Harry's purchase of it and 'Hedley' became Elsie's pet name for him.

Another Harry, Harry Woolley, was the brother of VAD Meg Woolley and the son of Thomas and Floria living at Sunnyside, the cottage on the Maidstone Road behind the Red Lion. Born in 1891, Harry was no longer living in Lenham when war broke out as he was running his own grocery shop in Watford (as well as working as a Post Office engineer). July 1915 was a life-changing month for him. On the 21st he married Elsie Whitelaw Coomber and a week later he enlisted for war service. Since 2007 Elsie had been boarding and working in Abbot's Langley in Hertfordshire at Leavesden Asylum, with a nursing certificate of the Medico-Psychological Association.

Harry's sister Meg, who was now working at Stanfield House hospital, must have paid Harry at least one visit to Watford for she had her photograph taken by a well known local photographer from St Albans, Herbert Birdsey. Harry's enlistment form shows that he was first assigned to join the Army Cyclists, but this was crossed out (perhaps when they discovered his work as a Post Office engineer!) and he served as a sergeant signaller in the Oxford and Buckinghamshire Light Infantry, becoming a despatch rider.

Harry Woolley during his service as a despatch rider

Two of his brothers were also serving. Thomas, aged 19, had been a telegraph messenger and enlisted for the Navy as a stoker. He served in HMS *Bulldog* during its mission to the Dardanelles to land troops on Gallipoli. During the patrol the destroyer struck a mine, but although damaged she survived. Harry's other brother, Robert, enlisted in 1915 for the Army Service Corps.

Harry and Elsie Woolley's wedding in July 1915. Meg is in the back row on the right, with her elder sister Nan (Annie) next to her in the middle. Betty is sitting next to Elsie.

Tom Woolley (junior) with his wife Doris in 1940

Harry Woolley *(left, front row)* during his war service

Harry's daughter Barbara marries Oliver Jones at St Mary's Church, Lenham, in 1942

Thomas Woolley (senior) with his family. At the back is his eldest daughter Nan (Annie). In the middle row are Floria and Thomas, flanked by their son Tom on the left and daughter Meg on the right. In front are Robert *(on the left)*, Arthur *(slightly behind in the middle),* young daughter Betty and Harry on the right.

Lester Edwin Smith was another volunteer. He was the son of George and Alice Smith, and was born in Herefordshire in 1898. By the time he enlisted in 1915, however, the family was living at Platts Heath, where his father was a grocer and butcher. Lester was only 17 in 1915 when he enlisted but nevertheless was serving in France. He had first joined the Royal Field Artillery and was then transferred to the 10th Battalion Cameronians (Scottish Rifles) which reached Boulogne in July 1915.

In October the Derby Scheme came into operation, which must have meant much anxiety for those of serviceable age and their families, all of whom would already be working for the war effort in other ways. George Post, an unmarried 22-year-old butcher living in Vine Cottages, Lenham, attested in November and when called up joined the Army Service Corps. Another to attest in November was Edward Fisher, the 20-year-old son of George, the farmer at Honywood Charity Farm in West Street on the downs. George lost his shepherd when in January Edward was called up to join the 3rd/4th Royal West Kent Regiment, a Territorial battalion engaged on training and guard duties. He fell ill with

Ted Fisher *(left)* with the handle of the shearing machine and Bob Ambrose shearing. The photograph was probably taken at Honywood Farm which Ted's father owned.

rheumatic fever in 1916 and was in hospital for three whole months, but was back with the battalion when it went to France in May 1917. He must have distinguished himself because he was promoted to acting lance corporal in December 1917, which was later confirmed.

Another George also attested just before Christmas. Farm labourer George Bugden was called up in February 1916. He was 24 and born in Liverton Street to John and Ellen Bugden. He joined the 8th Battalion Queens Royal West Surreys. George's older brother Walter had left home by the time war broke out. He was still single, 30 years old and was a carriage groom for William Stillwell at Surrenden Park, Pluckley, when he enlisted on 3rd April 1915 and joined the Army Service Corps. George and Walter do not seem to have been related to Charles William Bugden, veteran of the Boer War, whose story is told in Chapter 1.

John Morgan (not related to Jacob Morgan) was working for Andrew Barr at East Lenham Farm and was the son of John and Harriet of Water Street in Lenham Heath. When he signed up on 11th October aged 19, he was eager to join the Corps of Household Cavalry. His wish wasn't granted, however, and he was assigned instead to the 1st Life Guards, which had been heavily engaged at Loos, and was still on the Western Front when John joined them after training. They were in action again at the Battle of Arras.

Another Morgan from Lenham also served in the war, not thought to be related either to John or Jacob. This was Hazel Morgan (male!) who was the son of William and Ruth and in 1911 an assistant grocer, living at The Cottage, Lenham. He joined the London Scottish Regiment (14th London Regiment).

Thomas Love Golding enlisted on 9th December 1915, aged 22. He was then living in Faversham Road, and in 1911 had been working as a carter for a corn merchant, probably Lenham's L.J. Clark, when he was called up to the 2nd Scottish Rifles. William Golding (no known relationship with Thomas), was living in Liverton in 1911 when he was 33, and enlisted for the Royal Navy.

Another of the several Clark families in Lenham also lived in Faversham Road, in Lime Kiln Villas. Fred and Emma had five sons who served in the war. Edwin Jesse was the eldest at 31 in 1915; he was married to Daisy Lilian and living in The Limes. Jesse, as he was known, joined first the Suffolk regiment and later moved to the 2nd Battalion King's Own Yorkshire Light Infantry in France.

The next in age was William Leonard who was 27 in 1915. There are two William Clarks from Lenham on the Hatch list, one serving in the Royal West Kent Regiment, the other in the Royal Army Medical Corps. William Leonard must have been the William Clark in the Royal West Kents, as he was spotted by another Lenham man, Sam Clark, on his way to Mesopotamia in 1917 (see Chapter 3), where several of the Regiment's battalions served.

William's brother Joshua, aged 22, was working in one of the Lenham draper's shops, either Thomas Lurcock's, John Crump's or W.F. Hill's. Joshua joined the Royal Garrison Artillery. The fourth son, James Walter, was 21 and working as a wheelwright. He became a sergeant in the Royal Engineers, and the fifth son, Fred, aged 18, served with the Queen's Royal West Surreys.

By the end of 1915 the situation looked bleak for Britain. The evacuations from Gallipoli were taking place, the major offensives on the Western Front had failed once more leading to stalemate and on the Mesopotamian front Kut-al-Amara was under siege by the Turks from 4th December. Nor was the war at sea painting any more cheerful a picture. At home Zeppelin raids were still heavy. There had been six raids in September alone, with one over London bringing 120 casualties. After a brief lull, London was heavily hit in October with bombs hitting many targets in the Aldwych and Lincoln's Inn areas, and coming perilously close to Lenham when Dover and Tunbridge Wells were bombed. The same month brought the arrest and shooting of Edith Cavell in Belgium for aiding French and British fugitives, which caused outrage. Daily life was further affected with severe restrictions on alcohol consumption; the harvest had been above average, but prices of food were still rising.

In Lenham the newly built sanatorium on the downs was authorised in October to become the Lenham Sanatorium for the Treatment of Tubercular Canadian soldiers, and the VAD detachment at Stanfield House was steadily continuing its work with wounded soldiers. One of the patients was Fred Cox, who had been severely wounded in France. For Dr Temperley Grey every day must have been a reminder that his own son, John Grey, could well be the next to be called to the front.

Dr Temperley Grey supports the paralysed Fred Cox with VADs and patients outside Stanfield House

Though patriotism was still as strong, the mood of the bracing 1914 recruitment slogan of 'We don't want to lose you but we think you ought to go' was changing. Now songs such as 'Keep the Home Fires burning' summed up the general attitude. Letters home from the trenches reveal how much soldiers thought of home and how much they treasured letters and treats. At Christmastime a year earlier Lewis Hodgkin thanked his sister for the weekly paper she sent and added, 'Well, I expect you have got over Christmas by this time. ...I will let you know how I spent mine in a few weeks time. It won't be a very lively one this year.' Now, in Kut-al-Amara a year later, it was a far bleaker situation.

What happened to the men from Lenham

John, Frank, and Percy Barton: John died on 28th September 1915, at the Battle of Loos, and is commemorated on the Loos memorial. His twin Percy and brother Frank returned home safely from the Royal Army Ordnance Corps and Royal Engineers respectively, to their father Richard and his second wife Clara.

Charles Brakefield survived the war. Don Ambrose remembers him as living in Glover's Cottages, now the far side of the A20 from Lenham and so-called because the pub there, the Woodman's Arms, was run by a Glover. Charles Brakefield used to graze the goats from the farm on the common land opposite the cottages and lived a solitary life. As Don himself was a child when he knew him as an 'old man', it's not certain whether this is the Charles who fought in the war who would have been in his thirties or his father who would have been in his late sixties.

George and Walter Bugden: George's 8th Battalion fought at the Somme, where the fighting continued for many months after the offensive began in July 1916. George was killed on 29th December 1916. His brother Walter survived the war.

The Clark Brothers: James Clark survived the war, and probably returned to his former trade as a wheelwright. Edwin Jesse Clark was never able to return to Daisy and their son Ivan, for he was killed in France on 12th April 1918 during the First Battles of the Somme. Daisy remained in Lenham. William Leonard Clark survived the war as did James, Joshua, and Fred. Fred died during World War 2, and to a small boy he was remembered as 'an old man with a moustache' and to another as the man who 'always wore his cap at the back of his head'. He was the cricket club umpire for many years. At the beginning of the twentieth century there was a Fred Clark who ran a band for concerts and dances in Lenham and who might have been the father of the Fred who served in the war. Perhaps it was Fred Clark's band that played for the patients at the sanatorium. The Fred who served in the war was a friend of Sam Clark's (see Chapter 3) who recorded in his journal written in Mesopotamia that he had just written to him.

George Edward Coppins: George died in northern France with the 6th Battalion Royal West Kent Regiment on 27th February 1916. The Quarry cemetery where he is buried lies in a hollow of the Loos battlefield, and holds casualties from the Fosse and Hohenzollern Redoubt, two German strongpoints fiercely fought for during the Battle of Loos, so it may be that George died later of wounds received at the battle that had taken place in September 1915. He was aged 20.

Fred Cox: Although the summer of 1915 was a relatively 'quiet' time on the Western Front, the shelling and the fighting continued. Not long after he arrived in France, Fred was seriously wounded on 6th July 1915 by a German hand-grenade after taking a trench at Pilkem near Ypres. He lay with a shattered spine for nineteen hours before he was rescued. He was returned to Britain first to Netley hospital then to Dr Grey's care at the VAD hospital, but he remained paralysed from the waist down. Friends rallied round to help, and one gave him a donkey carriage. Dr Grey promptly approached the *Kent Messenger*, and in response to their appeal the matron of the isolation hospital at Tonbridge presented Fred with a donkey and other friends provided the wherewithal to buy the necessary harness (probably from Alfred Palmer in The Limes).

Fred Cox in his donkey carriage drawn by Ginny, his brother Frank *(standing)* and his young sister Bessie sitting beside Fred

Fred named the donkey Ginny and thereafter he, Ginny and the carriage were a familiar sight in Lenham. Fred lived for over five years, still suffering from great pain, but died on 10th March 1921 at the age of 28. He was given a funeral with full military honours in St Mary's church. The coffin was carried on a gun carriage from Chatham, and the donkey carriage was laden with flowers. Twelve Royal West Kent soldiers fired three volleys and their buglers played the Last Post. At Grove House, James Hatch flew the flag at half mast. When the plaque to the fallen was later unveiled in the church, a job that Fred had been too ill to undertake himself, it was his little sister Bessie who unveiled it. Her son Norbury was a valued contributor both to this book and to the village especially through his service to the St John Ambulance.

Frank and Percy Cox survived the war. Frank worked for the railways, and Percy later ran the Red Lion pub at Charing Heath.

Frederick Fellows was discharged from the army early in 1918, returning from France through wounds or ill health, having served there since May 1916. His condition seems to have improved as his pension was decreased from 27s. 6d. (£1.38) a week for the first month to 8s 3d (42p). He remained in Lenham, living first in Maidstone Road and then in Church Square.

Edward Fisher remained with the battalion until it was broken up in February 1918 and the company he was in, A Company, joined the 8th Battalion. In May he was serving in divisional reserve as a postman, perhaps because the rheumatic fever he had suffered earlier had weakened him. He was given a month's home leave in September, and as far as is known did not return to the front, but remained in Lenham.

Thomas Golding survived the war and returned to live in Cemetery Cottages. He came from a travelling family but settled in Lenham.

William Golding survived the war

Dr John Temperley Grey: Dr Grey came from Buckinghamshire to Lenham in the 1890s and was 48 when war broke out. His son John served in the war (see Chapter 3). After the war Dr Temperley Grey was awarded the OBE for his work at the VAD hospital, which he ran until it closed at the end of 1918. He continued to be the much respected and well liked GP for Lenham and Boughton Malherbe until his retirement in 1932, for which his grateful clients presented him with a commemorative book inscribed with all their names written in calligraphic script and beautifully illustrated. He died in 1935. His brother, Dr Thomas Campbell Grey, also came to live in Lenham in 1932 after his retirement from his Northumberland practice. His son Donald was also a doctor and settled in Harrietsham and another descendant of Dr Thomas still lives locally. Dr Temperley Grey himself was a motor car enthusiast and owned one of the first cars in Lenham.

Arthur Joy survived the war, and afterwards lived in Church Square in one of two cottages that were later demolished. The site is now a garden. He became an AA scout, in line with his former driving duties at Swadelands and his job during the war.

Percy Merton (Murton): Percy survived for less than a month after his arrival in France on 27th July 1915. He died on 25th August. On the Lenham memorial stone he appears as Murton. In census and military records Merton is often confused with Murton, but the War Graves Commission and regimental sites only list one casualty of either name: Percy Oliver Merton. By the time of his death his parents Henry and Emily had moved from Folkestone to Ashford. (Confusingly, there were two Percy Mertons in Kent born close together, but with different parents, Percy Oliver in Capel, and Percy S. Merton in Ashford – the latter at a different address to the one where Percy Oliver's parents lived at the time of his death.) A C. Murton also appears on the Hatch list, but could not be traced.

Gordon Mitchell remained in the army after the war as a captain, and lived with his family at Swadelands Manor until after the second world war. He had a son Harry and a daughter, and was a keen supporter of the village, being captain of the cricket team and, as Don Ambrose recalls, he provided 'glorious teas' after the matches. He also donated the ground for the bowls club and bequeathed much of the Swadelands estate to the village which allowed for the two schools to be built.

John Morgan survived the war and remained in the Lenham area.

Hazel Morgan survived the war.

Charles Ottaway survived the war. However the question is: which Charles Ottaway was this, father or son? Charles Alfred the father was a Sandway dealer before the war and 46 in 1915, rather old to be going off to war. Charles Alfred the son, however, was only 14 in 1915, which seems on the young side to be heading for the Balkans, although many young men did conceal their true ages. Whichever Charles Alfred it was, he was wounded early in 1917 and discharged from the army earlier than his comrades on 22nd November 1918, either because of his wound or because he fell sick (or even that his true age had been belatedly discovered – but that's sheer speculation).

George Post survived the war and remained in Lenham. He was one of Dr Grey's grateful patients who signed their names to his retirement present.

Lester Edwin Smith: died in action at Loos on 25th September 1915, after being in France just over two months. He is commemorated on the Loos memorial.

Earle and Arthur Viner: Earle survived the war but Arthur was killed in France on 3rd September 1918 while serving with the 7th Battalion Royal East Kent Regiment. Earle's battalion, the 11th Worcestershire Regiment, was suddenly ordered to Salonika in November 1915 and by the end of the war was in Bulgaria.

Richard Eric Rutland Webster survived the war, having married in February 1918 aged 31. No more is known of him, save that his family might have come over from Canada or the US in the late nineteenth century. His wife was working at the VAD hospital by the end of the war.

Frank Wickens: Frank died on 20th September 1915, shortly after his arrival at Gallipoli and is buried there in Lala Baba cemetery. The composite battalion in which he was serving and which included companies both from the Buffs and from the Royal West Kent Regiment has resulted in some records recording him as serving with the Buffs and others with the Royal West Kent Regiment.

Robert Wickens: Frank's brother Robert survived the war and worked at the family forge at 'Liberty Hall' in Grafty Green until his health gave way; he then worked for Gowers Garage, and later for Noakes of Ulcombe and Banks, the Harrietsham bakers.

George Wickens: their brother George survived the war, although wounded with the loss of an arm.

Albert Wiffen: Albert survived the war, although after Loos the 6th Battalion Royal West Kent Regiment was involved in heavy fighting at the Somme in 1916. Of the 617 men in action 375 became casualties. The following year the battalion was in another major battle at Arras, again in the autumn in the battles of Cambrai and in August 1918 at Morlancourt. However at some point Albert transferred to the Labour Corps, organised in 1917. He survived and returned to Kent, though his niece Beryl remembers that he was always thereafter 'not very well'. His sisters Dorothy and Daisy remained in the area. Daisy married Charles Smith from Egerton who had served during the war in the Buffs. They lived in Lenham where their daughter Beryl still lives.

Harry Wiffen, Albert's older brother by six years, also survived the war after a distinguished career as a sergeant serving in Egypt, for which he won a Meritorious Service Medal. Harry remained with the police after the war, living in the police station at Tunbridge Wells or Tonbridge. He must have returned to Lenham at some point however as Don Ambrose remembers what a wonderful goal runner he was. This was a game well known in East Kent, and was very popular because it could be played on any grass field, needing no equipment other than the players themselves. It was a team sport, played barefoot, and as the teams ran round the course they not only ran as hard as they could but had to avoid a 'Stroke' (touch) from the other team. Kicks were forbidden!

Harry Woolley returned to Lenham with his wife Elsie, who resigned from her Asylum work in 1917, and he became a highly valued village supporter. He worked as foreman for L.J. Clark & Co., the corn seed and coal merchants whose warehouse was in Station Yard; he was a member of the St John Ambulance, of the Buffaloes and of the bowls club, and very involved with the annual Lenham carnival. He, like Harry Wiffen, was an expert in goal running, and he also played cricket. In World War Two he joined the Observer Corps and taught cadets Aircraft Recognition using models and slides. He also taught morse code at his own home. He and Elsie, who died in 1946, had two sons and two daughters. During the Second World War the family took in many evacuees.

Patrick, the eldest son, served in the RAF from 1936 and retired as a wing commander. John (formally Francis John) died in Normandy after D-Day, during his World War Two service.

One of Harry's two daughters, Barbara, married Oliver Jones, during the Second World War, who was then serving in Royal Army Service Corps. Their wedding was a notable occasion. No bells were permitted, nor was there a choir. However, the procession was led by Fred Cox's teen-aged nephew Norbury, for which he was paid sixpence. His father promptly took it away, but years later Barbara returned it to him with interest. 'I haven't forgotten,' she

SERVICE MEDAL FOR MR WOOLLEY

Mr Robert Woolley, 5 Mains Drive, Dundee, has been awarded the Meritorious Service Medal.

A native of Kent, Mr Woolley is a civil executive officer with the army authorities at Balhousie Castle, Perth. He joined the Service Corps in 1915, and in his 24 years' army service he was in France and North and South China.

In 1939 he joined the Civil Service. After a spell in the Dundee Recruiting Office he was transferred to the Royal Engineers' Office in Dundee and Broughty Ferry. Later, he was promoted to Glasgow. He has been 18 months at Perth.

He was married in Hong Kong 24 years ago. Mrs Woolley, who was a nurse at a North China mission hospital, belongs to Downfield. Their daughter is a gym teacher at Logie Junior Secondary School, Dundee.

said. Harry Woolley stepped in to help run Lurcocks grocery during the war, and afterwards Oliver Jones too became a long time and much respected fixture behind the counter.

Meg Woolley: Meg remained in Stanfield House until the hospital closed at the end of December 1918, and later emigrated to Canada, where some time later she married a distant relative and went with him back to his native New Zealand to live. Meg's younger sister Betty had also trained as a VAD, although it is not known

KILLED BY ENEMY ACTION. — Mr. Thomas Woolley, ex-Leading Seaman, Torpedo Section, R.N., of Welling, Kent, son of the late Mr. T. W. Woolley, of Lenham, and Mrs. Woolley, of Blue Bell Hill, a brother of Mr. H. Woolley, of Sunnyside, Lenham, met with his death under tragic circumstances on April 20th. He and his wife were caught in an air raid and a bomb exploded near them killing both outright. Mr. Woolley, whose age was 45, was a native of Lenham, and joined the Navy at the age of 16 He took part in the last war and had a thrilling experience in the Dardanelles. his ship H.M.S. Destroyer "Bulldog," when assisting in the landing of troops at Gallipoli, was under intense fire from shore batteries and artillery, and had half of its hull blown away, but gallantly carried on with the remaining half until relieved. He also served on the China Station, at Malta and elsewhere. Since his retirement he had acted as agent for the British and Foreign Bible Society. The funeral took place at Bexley Heath on April 26th. The Pride of Welling Lodge, R.A.O.B., of which deceased was a member, held a Buffalo service at the graveside. At the weekly meeting of the Royal Lenham Lodge, R.A.O.B., on Tuesday last week, sympathy was expressed with Bro. H. Woolley, K.O.M., in his loss.

MR. T. WOOLLEY

for sure where she worked. However by the end of the war there are two Miss M. Woolleys listed in the VAD detachment records so it is probable that Betty was the second one. This is made even more likely as after the war Betty too emigrated to Canada and married in 1921. Her husband whom she had met in Lenham was a Canadian soldier.

Robert Woolley's career with the Royal Army Service Corps lasted 24 years and included service in France, China, and Hong Kong for which he received the Meritorious Service Medal. On leaving the army he joined the civil service at the Dundee recruiting office. While he was in Hong Kong he married a nurse at the north Chinese mission hospital.

Thomas Woolley: the third brother who joined the Navy stayed on there for some years ending his career as a leading seaman torpedo section. HMS *Bulldog* was sold for scrap in 1920, and its successor came to fame in the Second World War as the destroyer that captured an enigma machine which led to the deciphering of the code. Thomas's story has a tragic ending. Having survived the war, he moved to Welling in North Kent with his wife, and was killed by a bomb there in the Second World War.

Three

Soldiers in Line

From 'Tears' by Edward Thomas

By the beginning of 1916 it was clear that conscription was fast approaching and in Lenham as elsewhere the wounded and widows were an ever present reminder that war brought tragedy and grief. Women were now increasingly taking over jobs that had hitherto been presumed only suitable for men, notably in munitions factories. Bus conductors, tram drivers, train drivers, postwomen were but a few of the roles they now undertook. And then there was the land. Nearly half a million women were to be trained for a Women's Land Army. Others still sewed, knitted and cooked for the men at the front, including a consignment of plum puddings that were despatched to Gallipoli. Few there could have enjoyed them, with fighting and evacuations in progress.

In Lenham Stanfield House was fully operational and new staff were joining, including the vicar's wife, Mrs Etherington. Zeppelin raids were frequent and many now targeted Kent, particularly of course Dover and other coastal towns, including Ramsgate and Broadstairs, as well as Folkestone. The Kentish defences made a brave attempt at shooting one down, but so far no Zeppelins had been brought down anywhere in Britain and the raids continued. One on Liverpool in January killed 70 people.

On the Western front, the French began their offensive at Verdun in February, leaving the British to plan for their big offensive in the summer. On the Mesopotamian front, the last of the evacuated forces from Gallipoli reached it in January, but the siege at Kut-al-Amara continued. As one of Lewis Hodgkin's fellow soldiers, John Edward Sporle, later recorded: 'we were living like rats in the ground'. Rations were cut down and down, supplies failed to reach them, shelling continued day and day, casualties grew and sickness spread. On 29th April 1916 a communique conveyed the permission to capitulate, and the surviving forces, of which Lewis Hodgkin was one, were marched into Turkish captivity.

They were first forced to undergo a march of 100 miles to Baghdad where they were paraded with great glee of their captors, being stoned and spat upon. Then followed a death march of hundreds of miles. In the words of John

Sporle, they were 'kept without food, pushed and knocked about by our escort with whips and sticks. ... severe sickness set in amongst us prisoners'. Those too weak to continue were murdered by their captors. Their rations were eight ounces of flour mixed into river water.

The terrible conditions continued while the prisoners remained for several months in an Armenian church at Afion-Kara-Kisser, and were then forced onwards to Ada-Pazar where they were put to stonebreaking. It was probably during this period that Lewis Hodgkin succumbed to dysentery – though that could have been a cover-all cause of death – and he would probably have been one of the 300 of their number who died then and were buried by their comrades. This kind of life, being moved from one hovel to another, continued until the war ended. By that time out of the 2592 troops taken prisoner at Kut-al-Amara only about 850 survived, the rest having died either on the march or at the camps.

A postcard captioned underneath 'The Glorious First of July - our first prisoners'. By the time it was published however, the public would have known from casualty lists and the film of the Somme battle just how far the 1st July 1916 was from being glorious, but the brave face had to be maintained.

In the war at sea April saw the German bombardment of Great Yarmouth and Lowestoft, and at the end of May came the Battle of Jutland, the only sea battle of capital ships in the war. Both sides claimed victory, but the result was inconclusive. The British lost more ships than the German navy, including the

Black Prince on which Jacob Morgan had served, though not aboard when it sank. The battle did achieve something, in that the German capital fleet did not put to sea again. In June HMS *Hampshire* was lost and with it Field Marshal Kitchener, sparking off a spate of rumours that this was merely a ruse to fool the enemy or that he was away on a secret mission.

In April a tragedy took place closer to home for those in Lenham, when the Faversham munitions factory exploded on Sunday the 2nd, and killed 115 men. The cause was accidental, but it was a severe blow for Kent.

To counteract the sombre news entertainment flourished with a vast increase in London nightclubs, shows such as *Chu Chin Chow* which opened on 3rd August and ran for five years with full houses, and a dancing craze with jazz clubs flourishing. The older generation became aghast at the frivolous ways of the young. The Lenham Village Institute must have been busy with concerts, travelling theatre shows, and – of course – cinema shows, by now coming into their own with both UK and US films ranging from Shakespeare to Charlie Chaplin and the Keystone Cops. There was already a thriving network of established cinemas in Kent. The former skating rink in Pudding Lane, Maidstone, had turned to films, and another cinema thrived in Earl Street. Ashford too had an Electric Picture Palace. Amongst a wide choice, this year the actor Sir John Martin Harvey, famous for portraying Sydney Carton from Dickens' *A Tale of Two Cities* on the stage, would be wowing audiences with a romantic British film *Broken Melody* and from the US were coming the first films of the dashing Douglas Fairbanks (senior).

Thomas, the father of the Chambers brothers in Lenham Heath

But entertainment could not mask the fact that more and more men were now being called up for the war. There were two families with the name of Chambers in Lenham at the time, one living at the Red Lion, and the other at Chapel Mill House in Lenham Heath. Here lived Thomas and Ellen Chambers, their sons George, Frederick, Edward and Bertie and their daughter Rosie. Three daughters, Mabel, Alice and Elizabeth, were already married.

Three of Thomas's four sons fought in the war. The oldest of them was George, who was 32 in 1916 and served with the 17th Battalion, The Duke of Cambridge's Own (Middlesex) (1st Football) Regiment. Next came Fred who

Fred Chambers

was 31. He served first with the 11th Royal Sussex, then the Lincolnshire and finally the Welsh Regiment. Then came Edward who was 19 and was still working on a farm when George wrote to him from the front in September 1916. Then Edward served in the Royal Marine Light Infantry. The youngest Chambers son, Bertie, who was 15, was too young to serve in the forces but must have been invaluable as a farm worker.

George's battalion had reached France in November 1915, but judging by a letter he sent back to his married sister Alice Foreman who preserved them all, George seems to have joined it in July 1916. By now the Somme offensive had begun. He wrote to her on the 25th:

My dear Sister just a line to let you know that I am allright and hope
you are the same we are having some nice weather out here there is
about 600 of us going up the firing line to day to have a look at the
germans I dont know weather I shall come back again or not but I will
make the buggers jump if I get side of them dont let mother know that
I am going or else she will worry over it I will write and let you know
what it is like I dear say it is like hell up there but we shall haft to get
use to that all my mates are going. … so good luck to you all
With love to you all

What lay ahead for George would have been the battle of Delville Wood, in which George's battalion, in 2nd Division, fought as part of the Somme offensive. As the first major offensive at the Somme had failed so disastrously, particular targets were picked out such as this wood. The operation proved a British success, but the losses on both sides were high. George did 'come back' as he doubted in his letter, but more fighting lay ahead. By November, the offensive was beginning to draw to its close for the winter, and by now his confidence in making 'the buggers jump' was still less gung-ho.

On the 17th he wrote home:

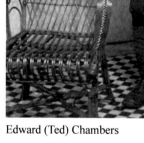

Edward (Ted) Chambers   Thomas's wife Ellen *(seated)*

My dear Sister and Brother just a line in answer to your letter and parcel you must excuse me for I had to borrow this letter to write because we ant got our packs yet well I hope you are allright as it leaves me the same but we have had a pretty hot time lately I daresay you will see it in the papers before you get this letter but I manage to scarpe out of it without a scratch so I was lucky but some of my mates did not it was very hot time.

George's letter had been written in the middle of the Battle of the Ancre from 13th to 18th November, in which the 2nd Division was involved. It was the last big attack by the British before the winter weather struck, and there was heavy fighting. He wrote in a letter just before it began: 'We got plenty of clothing, but not enough grub.'

Mabel and Lizzie, two of the
Chambers brothers' sisters

Bertie Chambers, younger brother of Fred, George and
Edward

All his letters and others by the men of Lenham reveal the great importance of the arrival of letters and newspapers from home, and express their constant thoughts of what might be going on in Lenham while they were away. The letter written on the 17th continues:

> well I must thank you very much for the parcel I have just open it I
> thought there might be a bit of writing paper and envelope in it but I
> ant had time to try them yet but look out when I do it wont be long
> before tea is up and then I will have a go at them mother said she sent
> a parcel but I have not received them …we have done some very good
> work so you will see by the papers well we are having some better
> weather now it as started freezing now pretty hard this morning and pretty
> nippy to not very hot for filling the worsel carts is it have you done the
> thrashing yet or [?] . . . now have they done that other bridge I want it
> done by the time I come home I don't know when it will be but I should
> think they will let us have some leave this winter . . . well I must finish
> with love to you all from your loving Brother GC Thank you for the
> parcel.

weather out here there is about 600 of us going up to the firing line to day to have a look at the germans I dont know weather I shall come back again or not but I will make the buggers jump if I get side of them

dont let mother know that I am going or else she will worry over it I will write and let you know what it is like I dear say it is like hell up there but we shall haft to get use to that all my mates are

A page from George Chambers' letter home written on 25th July 1916. He would have been joining the front line at the Somme.

Although there were several Clark families in Lenham who sent their sons to war, the best known today is probably Samuel Clark's family from Church Square, where he lived with his wife Maria, brought up their large family and ran his building company. His family included seven sons, Frank who was 39 by the time war broke out, Herbert who was two years younger, George who was 35, Samuel (junior) who was 33, Percy who was 31, Arthur 28 and Louis (sometimes spelled Lewis in records) 21.

By the census of 1911, Samuel (senior) was 55, and only Arthur, Louis and their daughter Lily were living at home. Sam (junior) was working for the family firm, but living in the High Street and married to Sarah; they had a young son, Samuel Wilfred, and daughters, Sybil and Doris. He enlisted for the Royal Engineers at Maidstone in 1916, aged 35 and after six months training at Detling left Chatham (complete with his newly issued Pay Book with a princely credit of £2) for Devonport on 28th April 1917.

Six days later they steamed away from Britain and arrived in India in July. To his pleasure, in Bombay harbour he spotted Frank Todd from Lenham

Sam Clark in the Royal Engineers

(see Chapter 5). Three days later Sam was on his way by ship to Basra in Mesopotamia. 'God it is hot,' he wrote on 7th August, having disembarked the day before at the base of Ashar. This is where he saw another familiar face. 'In the evening I felt a bit sick. Oh, I saw W.L. Clark.' (This must have been William Leonard Clark, the son of Fred and Emma, serving with the Royal West Kent Regiment.)

After they disembarked, they were fighting disease not yet the Turks, and had orders to stay in their huts between 10am and 4pm. 'It's hot enough to smother you in there.' By 22nd August 1917 a third of the force were in hospital with fever. Sometimes they had to be 'carried off parade'. Sam himself fell sick and had periodic bouts in hospital.

Sam remained at Ashar for some while, having first expected to head for Basra and then go by river to Kut, now back under British control. Post was delayed with no post or parcels arriving or leaving – the mail ship had been sunk, together with Sam's 'silks for the children' that he had sent home. In September a parcel at last arrived but in the meantime the cake had gone stale – a big disappointment. Then he, like many of his fellow servicemen, fell

Arthur *(left)* and Louis *(right),* two of Sam Clark's brothers

Sam Clark as a young man

Sam Clark at 90

sick. Later in the month life cheered up: 'I have got my discharge from hospital today and only hope I get back with the boys again. My baby Doris's birthday!'

Five of Sam's brothers were in the forces, as were some of their children. Frank Clark, the eldest of Sam Clark's (senior) sons, seems to have moved away from the village, but the next in age, Herbert, had married and settled here. His son Hubert was 18 in 1916, and served in the Sherwood Foresters. Hubert's brother Percy also served in the war. George Clark, the next of Sam Clark senior's sons in age to Herbert, served in the Royal Garrison Artillery. After Samuel junior, came Percy, the uncle of the Percy mentioned above (the son of Herbert). He was 33 in 1916, and served as a sergeant in the army, either in the Machine Gun Corps or the Queen's Royal West Surreys. (The reason for the doubt is that it is not certain which of the two Percys served in which regiment.)

Another of Sam Clark senior's sons was Arthur, who in 1911 had married Ethel Freed. She was an assistant to John Farmer, owner of a butcher's shop in Lenham Square. Jessie Neaves was one of the witnesses at the wedding (probably the former Mrs Renwick from Top Hill Farm (see Chapter 5). With Arthur away

The Three Sams: Old Sam, Young Sam and Young Sam's son Sam. 'Old Sam' was the Sam Clark who went to Mesopotamia.

Arthur Clark

in the Royal Marine Engineers, Ethel might have found her metier as a VAD in Stanfield House, although the Mrs E. Clark on its VAD list could well have been Emma Clark, Fred's wife from Lime Kiln Cottages or even Mrs Ernest Clark.

Samuel and Maria had one more son who served in the war. Louis was 23 in 1916, and joined the Royal Army Medical Corps. He must have been serving in Mesopotamia as he came to see his brother Sam several times when he was stationed there.

Lancashire Batteries of the Royal Field Artillery gathered in Lenham Square

Also from Lenham Square came Charles Day, who was a trooper in the Royal East Kent Mounted Rifles (Yeomanry) and then transferred to the East Kent Regiment. The son of Frederick and Adeline Day, Charles was 19 in 1916, and a grocer's clerk. His father was well known in Lenham and one of the first trustees of the Hatch Charity. His wife Adeline was a VAD at Stanfield House.

The Reverend Francis McDonald Etherington, the vicar of Lenham when war broke out, had come to the village to replace the Reverend George Garnier who had left early in 1914 to move to Garboldisham Rectory near Thetford. George Garnier was married and 35 when he enlisted at the end of 1915, and served not as a chaplain but in the Army Service Corps Mechanical Transport unit. He survived the war.

His successor Francis Etherington had been vicar of Minehead before coming to Lenham. In 1916 he was 44 years old, with a wife, two daughters and a young son, who later in life also went into the church. Francis Etherington had replaced George Garnier as a trustee of the Hatch Charity but quickly had to resign himself because by 1916 he was already in Egypt serving as a chaplain to the forces.

Many households in Lenham were affected by conscription, either seeing their sons still being called up under the Derby Scheme or waiting tensely for the call-up papers they knew must be coming once conscription became a legal fact in May. For some of the many men on the Hatch list however, it has not been possible to find out in which year they enlisted. One of these is Alfred Robinson, a fruit picker, the son of George and Mary and living in Sandway. He was serving in the Grenadier Guards. Another is Robert Tanton who was 20 in 1916, and the only son of his widowed mother Matilda, who had moved with her husband Robert from Norfolk and now lived in the Square. He had been a coal merchant, a business that his widow carried on from their home at Wickham House. She sold the coal through the side door. By age 15 Robert junior was already at work as an assistant draper and living in Week Street, Maidstone. He served as a corporal in the King's Royal Rifle Corps.

Another one whose enlistment date is unknown is William John Bushrod who was 26 in 1916. Born in Doddington, he was living in West Street with his wife Minnie and working as an agricultural labourer. He joined the Royal Navy as a stoker.

Stanley Terry from Rose Cottage in Lenham Heath had attended school in Charing Heath and by 1911 was a baker's assistant. His father James drove traction engines. In 1916 he was 22, and had been in France since 1st June 1915 with the 6th Battalion the Buffs. In September, this battalion had faced heavy fighting at the battle of Loos and again at the Hohenzollern Redoubt strongpoint in early 1916. Stanley was promoted to corporal. There were several Terry households in the parish of Lenham at the time, but Stanley is not known to have been related to the other Terrys on the Hatch list.

Arthur Town (not known to be related to Albert Town who was also on the Hatch List) was born in 1894. He was the son of George and Christiana Town, who by 1911 was twice widowed, having been first married to Joseph Bolton, with whom she had three sons, two of whom served in the war. Arthur was working as an agricultural labourer in Platts Heath, when he attested in February 1916, and in July was posted first to 6th Battalion Royal West Kent Regiment, and almost immediately sent to the 7th which was fighting at the Somme and needed reinforcements.

Many Smiths from Lenham appear on the Hatch list, and one of them is

William Smith. However, in the 1911 census there are two Williams who would have been of serviceable age, one two years younger than the other. The most probable of the two to have been on the list was the son of a farmer cum wood-cutter, William, and his wife Adelaide who in 1911 were living in School Cottages, Lenham. (They had another son too, George, and as there are three George Smiths on the Hatch list one of them must have been William's brother, probably the one who signed up in December 1914 aged 18 (see Chapter 6).

William enlisted on 21st October 1916, aged 27. He had once been a gamekeeper, but by 1916 he was a gardener. He had married May Peters only a year earlier, and they were living at Cemetery Cottages. He joined the 8th (Cyclist) Battalion, a Territorial battalion under the aegis of the Essex Regiment on home defence duties.

Bernard Lampard was also in the Essex regiment, and became a lance corporal in the 9th Battalion in the 12th (Eastern) Division, which faced heavy fighting at the Somme. There were Lampards living in Lenham at least from the 1880s and up until the late 1950s, when a married couple was living in High House (now Honywood House). The husband served in the Royal Observer Corps during the Second World War. Bernard, however, cannot be connected in census reports to any of them. He appears on the 1891 census as a three-year-old living with his grandparents, William and Ruth Coast, in Sandway. Ten years later the census shows him living in Wanstead in a school cum orphanage. Ten years after that, in 1911, he is a 23-year-old boarder in Clapham working as a bookkeeper, but by the time he enlists he was living in Bognor where his mother had remarried. He reached France on 24th August 1915.

Albert Wickens was not from the same family as the Wickens brothers of Chapter 2, Frank, George and Robert. He was the son of Alfred and Frances Wickens, born in Boughton Malherbe and working on his father's farm at Elmstone. He was 35 in 1916 and served as a gunner with the Royal Garrison Artillery.

Church Square became even emptier when John Uden the chimney sweep signed up. He was 36 in 1916, and enlisted on 15th February to serve in the 5th Essex Regiment. This battalion had been at Gallipoli but was in Alexandria by 1916. John Uden was born in Petham and married to Alice with a son William John. He was a familiar face in Lenham in days when chimney sweeps were essential for every household.

Church Square had also seen the birth of Walter Clifton years earlier (no known relation of George Clifton). He was born there in 1876 to fishmonger James and his wife Sarah. Walter had left Lenham behind him however. By 1901 he was working as a servant to John and Ida Wizner in Stone Street, Maidstone and ten years later he had moved to London with his wife Lilian and small daughter Gertrude to take up a position as butler. By the time he joined the army on 28th July 1916, however, he was a butcher in the Fulham Road, having enlisted when he was forty, almost at the age limit of 41. He joined the Royal Garrison Artillery, 341st Siege Battery.

Other parents to face a son's departure included Dr Temperley Grey and his wife Bertha, now living in a cottage while the doctor ran the VAD detachment. Their son John had been born in Shipley, Yorkshire, and was 18 in 1916. He served with the 7th Battalion Royal West Surreys, which had been in France since July 1915 in 18th Division.

Arthur 'Pop' Hambley, the signalman at the railway station, also had to bid au revoir to his son, Victor, who was living with him in Chipperfield House in the High Street (its whereabouts are not known). Victor was working as a clerk when he enlisted at twenty-one and he joined first the 8th London Regiment and then the Labour Corps.

From Sandway Absalom Beaney left home for the forces in 1916 when he was 34. He was a farm labourer, the son of Henry, who was a licensed hawker, and his wife Phoebe. Absalom seems to have been their only son, but in 1911 there were six daughters at home in Liverton Street. Absalom served in the Hampshire Regiment.

Another loss to Church Square was Albert and 'Ma' (as she was known)

John Hughes, Lenham's postmaster, in dress uniform

Brown's son Edward. Edward was born at Wormshill on the downs in 1898, and probably served with the Royal West Kent Regiment and later the Sherwood Foresters and Derbyshires.

George Offen was a farm labourer too. He was living in Woodside Green in 1911, the son of Edwin and Minnie at High Ash Cottage. There was a farmer at West Street called Alfred Offen so that might be the farm where George worked. George joined the Essex Regiment.

A huge gap occurred in village

John Hughes in the Royal Field Artillery

life when John (Jack) Hughes from Lenham Post Office signed up. From assisting his father in his boot-repairing business, Jack succeeded Walter Record at the village post office (then in the High Street) and then bought the old Hussar pub on the corner of the High Street and Lenham Square in which to run it. In 1911, when he was 24, he had married Mabel Vallance in Weymouth. His father James kept a shoe repair shop, but by the time war broke out owned a greengrocery store across the Square. Jack Hughes served as a driver in the Royal Field Artillery. His younger brother Harold, seven years younger than Jack, served in the 4th East Surrey Regiment.

The war situation at the end of 1916 was bleak after the disastrous losses at the Somme, which had been rammed home in Britain not only by the sombre listings in the newspapers of the war dead but by actual scenes shot at the Somme front in a film shown at cinemas, a bold step forward by the Government. The servicemen never talked of their experiences outright in letters home for obvious reasons, but now with their own eyes their families and friends in Britain at least had some inkling of what was happening. Nor was there yet good news from the other war fronts, nor good news on the war at sea – nor yet any sign of the

John Hughes *(front row, far left)* in the Royal Field Artillery

USA joining the war. Zeppelin raids continued although there was at last hope – or so it seemed. The first Zeppelin had been shot down in England, shortly followed by three more in September. The morale boost was enormous to Britain. At the end of December, the prime minister, Asquith, famed for his 'wait and see' policy, had been replaced by David Lloyd George, a far more vigorous figure who believed in action.

What happened to the men from Lenham

Absalom Beaney survived the war and returned to Lenham, where he lived at the back of the former sanatorium on the downs, now the site of Highbourne Park housing development.

Edward Brown returned to Lenham and his father's Pond Farm which he inherited. After he sold the farm to what is now Lenham Storage, he went to live with his sister until his death in 1975. He never married, but the family still live locally.

William John Bushrod survived the war and returned to Lenham. He died in 1936 and is remembered as having lived in Vine Cottages with his son.

George Chambers: 'You never know your luck till the ball has done rolling', he had written home on 18th April 1917. It was his last letter for ten days later George was killed in action, probably at the Battle of Arleux, which took place on the 28th to the 29th April. It was addressed to his sister Alice, who treasured it thereafter, and it began:

The present George Chambers, son of Bertie, during his national service in Kenya

The present George Chambers during his national service

My dear Sister and Brother just a line in answer to your kind letter
hoping this one will find you all quite well as it leaves me the same
at the present yes we are having some very funny weather and here
snowing and hail and then it is terrible for our job cant get on with
the busins well we had better weather at Chrismas time I expect thay
cant get on with the garden you must put in a good lot of taters this
year for I think thay are getting pretty short & them papers form Mother
this night [?] thay seem to give a pretty good account of it dont they it ant
so easy as it looks in the paper thay are a artfull lot oh so Fred [his
brother] thinks he wont go just yet dose he but thay wont keep him long
after thay give you your 4 days if he ant done his taring he can do it out here

George did his best to keep in touch with everyone and send home what little gifts he could. He anxiously enquires in several letters whether a lace handkerchief that he sent to his sister arrived. It did. It was found folded up with his last letter.

Frederick Chambers survived the war. George had written in a letter home in November 1916, 'I think that Fred as got a better job and good luck it don't look as if he is coming out here yet,' and in December he joked, 'I had a letter from Fred last week and it was time for he is a bad writer.'

Edward Chambers survived the war but died young of his injuries in 1932. George enquired after his brother in a letter of October 1916: 'how dose ted kept on with the sheep I expect he is in the fold again up to his ass in muck and water but that is better than this job' and in another letter: 'has he took any prizes yet?'

Samuel Clark (junior): remained on the Mesopotamian front until 1919. In the autumn of 1917, when at last the British were gaining the upper hand, he recorded: 'The Commandant gave us news of a success on the Euphrates by Brooking's column; we took over 200 prisoners and 4 guns, and prisoners giving up everywhere. The Turkish commander also taken so it bucked us up a bit.' They needed bucking up, overcome with heat and fever. One soldier committed suicide.

During his service in Mesopotamia Sam suffered much ill health from fever. He still recorded the good news of the war's end however. On 2nd October 1918 there was 'news of unconditional surrender of Bulgaria', two days later came good news from the Palestine front which had opened up in 1917, and of the Anglo-Arab 'capture of Damascus with 9,000 Turks,' on 4th October 1918.

On 16th October Sam recorded seeing Turkish prisoners himself: 'A batch of Turkish prisoners went past this morning, about 700 of them.' On 9th

From the diary kept by Sam Clark during his service in Mesopotamia

November they had heard that 'the whole [German] navy has mutinied and that little doubt felt in London that owing to the military situation and internal trouble in Germany that they will surrender.' The following day he simply records: 'Went to Ramadan' and on the 11th came the big news: 'We heard that the Germans surrendered unconditionally' – not technically true but the armistice had indeed come into force. 'I long to get home,' he wrote. That was not to happen for some

Sam Clark with his wife Sarah and grandchildren. Next to Sam is Godfrey Tappenden, the son of Sam and Sarah's daughter Sybil. Standing at the back is Janet Clark (now Janet Humphrey), daughter of their son Sam. At the front is John Stuart, son of their daughter Doris, and next to Sarah is Sam, Janet's brother, the son of Sam's son Sam.

time. He did not reach England until September 1919.

Sam returned to Sarah, his children and the family building business. He and Sarah had three children, Sam, Doris and Sybil, whose own children are as active in Lenham life today as Sam himself was. He died much loved and respected aged 92 in 1972.

His sister Lily had married William Boorman (see Chapter 5), but had no surviving children. *Arthur Clark* returned to Lenham and the family business, becoming the local undertaker. He and Ethel had no children. *Hubert Clark* also returned safely to Lenham, as did his brother Percy and the other Clark brothers, *George, Percy* and *Louis.* Today's Lenham has much to thank Louis for, for his son was the well known Michael Clark, married to Betty, and their son Gez is now Lenham's town crier and taxi driver.

Walter Clifton did not survive the war. He returned to Lilian and Gertrude having been wounded or fallen ill, and died aged 47 on 20th February 1917. He is buried in Lenham Cemetery.

Charles Frederick Day survived the war and lived at Westwood Court (since demolished).

Etherington, Francis McDonald: Captain Etherington returned on leave to Lenham on at least one occasion in April 1918, and took the service for the death of a Canadian soldier in the Lenham Sanatorium. His curate the Reverend P.M. Taylor had taken over his role during his absence, and played an active role in the village. The Reverend Etherington returned to Lenham but left Lenham in 1921.

John Grey was honourably discharged from the army because of disability in June 1918. He married Elizabeth, a physiotherapist who worked at the Lenham sanatorium, and they had one daughter, Bertha, known as Birdie. John died in 1927.

Victor Hambley was called up in November 1916, survived the war and was discharged in March 1919. Afterwards he ran the White Horse pub in Sandway for many years, during which it became famous for its cricket games that were organised in its meadow. His wife was a Londoner by birth and through her contacts teams came down from the capital to play there. Other teams were those from the Red Lion and L.J. Clark team. Victor was a busy man. Not only was he running the White Horse, but he also acted as landlord for Lord Chilston. He was a good businessman, obviously, because he collected the tenants' rents at the White Horse, and once a year treated them to a free pint.

Harold Hughes survived the war and went to run a smallholding in Egerton.

John (Jack) Hughes returned to Lenham Post Office, and he and his descendants served Lenham well for many decades. His daughter Esme Brown ran it after John, and she was followed by her sister Jean's husband Bill Peter, whose father had a distinguished First World War record (see Chapter 6). Bill himself served in the Royal Fusiliers during World War 2.

Jack Hughes's father James probably continued to run the greengrocery (in what is now part of Pippa's Tearooms) for some years after the war until his death in 1925. Either then or earlier it was taken over by his daughter Hilda. As well as running the post office, Jack also farmed a smallholding, where he grew fruit including strawberries, which his daughter Jean recalls taking to the station for rail transport to Covent Garden. Jack Hughes died in July 1944, a great loss to the village.

Bernard Lampard

Bernard Lampard does not appear on the Lenham war memorial but is remembered in the cemetery with a poppy on Armistice Day each year. Bernard died on 13th August 1916 at the Somme by a shell landing close to him, and is remembered on the Thiepval Memorial. His mother had remarried after the death of her husband, also a Bernard, and became Mrs J.E.Smurthwaite. She was still living in Bognor.

George Offen survived the war and returned to Lenham. He lived on Lenham Hill Road, where his family continued to work on the land.

Alfred Robinson was killed in action in the 2nd battalion Grenadier Guards on 29th April 1916, aged 23. He is buried in Calais, presumably having died in one of the base hospitals.

William Smith was discharged from the army in February 1917 because of sickness.

Robert Tanton: A corporal in the 1st London Rifles, Robert was killed in action on 22nd March 1918, aged 22. His mother Matilda continued to run the coal business and also let apartments for many years after the war. Another Tanton (not related as far as is known) was the miller at Lenham Heath, and his son figures in George Chambers' letters as serving abroad, although he was not on the Hatch list.

Stanley Terry died on 17th March 1916, thought to have been killed by an aerial torpedo. Aerial torpedoes were being developed for naval use, but in the trenches the word seems to have been used more loosely to mean German *Minenwerfer* rounds or trench mortar shells.

Arthur Town was involved in the heavy fighting at the Somme for about three months until he was wounded on 2nd November, losing a leg. He was unlucky indeed because on that day his battalion was only just moving up to the line and not in action, but such troop movements were often targeted by the enemy. Arthur was sent back to Blighty (soldier's slang for their homeland) and was officially discharged on 13th March 1918, receiving a pension of 16s a week for life (80p). He married Amy and became a steward at the Working Men's Club, now the Lenham Social Club, and continued to live at Sandway. His son Fred worked for Clarks the builders as a painter.

John Uden returned to his wife and children, continuing his chimney sweeping career and moving from Church Square to the Ashford Road. His story has a sad ending, because he died in an accident with his cart in 1943 in Lenham High Street. Their 'dear son William John', it is recorded on the Uden tombstones in the cemetery, had died four years earlier, also after an accident.

Albert Wickens survived the war.

Four

No Tears Left

From 'Tears' by Edward Thomas

Nineteen seventeen saw the war biting ever deeper on the military fronts. On the Western Front the Battle of Arras offensive began on 9th April, during which many men from Lenham were lost, as was the poet Edward Thomas. He died on the first day, Easter Monday. The opening battle was the struggle for Vimy Ridge, fought by four divisions of Canadian troops and successful at great sacrifice. The whole offensive was also successful but it still failed to achieve the essential breakthrough. March brought revolution to Russia, in April America finally declared war on Germany and China too at last joined the war. A world war became just that, although the impact of the American effort was not to be felt for another year. Meanwhile the summer was to see another major British offensive, the Third Battle of Ypres, which was still raging in November.

The home front too was under great pressure. The new government under Lloyd George faced severe problems. In February German policy took a new turn: to starve Britain into surrender by using its submarine force to sink merchant shipping, with the result that every piece of spare land in Britain became a target for growing food, not just for farmers and smallholders, but everyone. The Ministry of Food had been set up in mid December under its Food Controller, as a voluntary campaign of rationing was failing. Milk was the first item to be controlled, and sugar ration cards issued. Conscription had intensified the problem of the drainage of labour from the lands, and although now essential workers were exempt the earlier rush of volunteers had taken its toll.

However 1917 was to see the first organised governmental use of women for labour, beginning with the Women's Land Army. This was followed by the Women's Royal Naval Service and in March by the Women's Army Auxiliary Corps intended to free soldiers from the rear service areas for the front by replacing them with women. It included a motor transport section. In April the first service women were sent to France.

Side by side with the use of women workers in rear and base areas on the fighting fronts, the Labour Corps emerged this year as a separate force by amalgamating the existing labour battalions of the Army Service Corps, Royal Engineers and Pioneers. By the end of the war it accounted for over ten per cent of army servicemen and increasingly they were working on or by the front line. Men from the British Empire swelled its ranks, as did many from China after it joined the war. Many of those who had enlisted from Lenham were sent or transferred to the new corps.

On the home front, the Zeppelin threat tailed off, but was replaced by an even greater one, as the German Gotha aircraft began their bombing campaign which began in May, including a devastating attack on Folkestone in which 71 people were killed. The same raid killed 18 soldiers at Shorncliffe, 16 of them Canadians. Many more were wounded in both places, again mostly Canadians in Shorncliffe.

As the author Mrs Dorothy Peel wrote in 1929, by this time of the war Britain was 'a country of women, old men, young boys, and children with a sprinkling of men in khaki.' Lenham was no exception. Every family in the parish of Lenham would see someone either under their roof or otherwise close to them leave for service. Since the public showing of the film of the Somme there had been more awareness of what sons and husbands were going through. The Government seized the opportunity to issuing public information films, as they were called, most of them very short, two to ten minutes, some based on cartoon images to help ram home appeals for people to buy National War Savings Certificates or War Bonds mixed with newsreel material of war scenes or fictional representations, such as of Edith Cavell's death. A two and a half minute film featured the comedian George Robey drawing a caricature of himself purchasing Savings Certificates at a post office, and *John Bull's Animated Sketchbook* revealed an artist's moving hand as he illustrated popular jokes and caricatures of comedians like Charlie Chaplin.

To counterbalance the bleakness of the military situation and daily life, entertainment took an even more important role in boosting morale. London theatres were packed with servicemen on leave, not just British but with New Zealanders, Australians, Canadians and others of the then Empire's forces. Number one show from 1916 was *The Bing Boys Are Here*, with the comedian George Robey and his co-star Violet Loraine, which was a cross between a revue and a play portraying London life. Their hit song was 'If you were the only girl in the world'. It ran for months, and with the US now joining the war it was followed a short while later by *The Bing Boys on Broadway,* at the Alhambra in Leicester Square. Musical plays drew large audiences including the ever popular *Chu Chin Chow*. Sales of sheet music for popular wartime songs flourished, as

BRITISH SOLDIERS IN THE SOMME MENDING A ROAD.

Wartime postcard in aid of the YMCA Hut Fund, showing British soldiers in the Somme repairing a road. In 1917 the Labour Corps was formed. The YMCA Hut Fund provided refreshment and recreation for soldiers in the UK and in France, both at major centres and at the front. In mid-1915 it set up a hostel for relatives visiting the wounded in France. Women were amongst those killed while working at the front in the Huts, and one was awarded the Croix de Guerre avec palme.

did the cinema.

The troops also had entertainment, both at the front and while on leave. The Fovant training camp, chiefly known now for the regimental badges that the recruits cut into the hillsides, boasted its own Garrison Cinema. The actress Lena Ashwell pioneered taking concerts and plays to hospitals and the front line forces in France, Malta, Egypt and Palestine, and although the government were not interested, the YMCA sponsored the initiative. Its success led to an established official unit, ENSA, in the Second World War. No less than 600 artists were involved, both men and women, including such names as Sir John Martin Harvey and Lilian McCarthy. At home such stars as the beautiful Ellaline Terriss sang songs such as 'Thank you for all you're doing', to an appreciative audience of troops on leave. The YMCA ran a hut scheme like the NAAFI in World War 2, which supplied tea, coffee, buns, writing paper, ink, stamps, and pens to the men by day and by night and both at the front and at home on leave. The huts gave them space to write letters home, thump out tunes on the piano and generally relax.

Entertainment whether outside the village or in the Village Institute

DOUGLAS FAIRBANKS.

The dashing film star Douglas Fairbanks at the beginning of his career

From early 1915 to 1919 the actor Lena Ashwell organised over 600 actors, singers and musicians to entertain the men at the front and in hospitals in France, Malta, Egypt and Palestine.

Comedian George Robey and his co-star Violet Loraine in the show popular with the forces *The Bing Boys Are Here*

Ellaline Terriss, the darling of London musical theatre who sang for the troops on leave in London

William Chapman, the Lenham Heath butcher, with his son Leslie and Leslie's son. Leslie's half brother William served in the Royal East Kent Yeomanry during the war.

was a welcome relief for Lenham in its efforts to attack the food shortage, cope with rationing and fill the gaps in its labour force. Among the latter was the postal service; Sandway, to take just one instance, now had a postwoman. It all helped the feeling of a united front against 'Kaiser Bill', demonised as the cause of all Britain's woes.

The drainage on manpower leached remorselessly onwards. William Chapman was the son of the William Chapman, who was the Lenham Heath butcher, buying in and slaughtering the cattle. He had three daughters and in 1914 just the one son William, who served in the Royal East Kent Mounted Rifles (Yeomanry) during the war.

Not related, as far as is known, to William, although also linked to Lenham Heath, was 26-year-old Bertie Friend Chapman, who served as a lance corporal in the Buffs. He was the son of the widowed Ellen Chapman, and had been born in East Lenham, but was working away from home. In 1911 he was a boarder at a farm in Bobbing, near Sittingbourne, and by the time he enlisted on 7th December 1915 he had moved to Herne Bay, and his mother too had moved. She was living in Ashford. In 1915 he was working as a fireman on motor tractors. In this he might have been encouraged by his father, Albert, who in 1901 had been driving them at Marshalls Farm in Lenham Heath.

There were other Chapmans who served in the war. One was Frederick Chapman. There are several Fred Chapmans in the census records with connections to Lenham Heath, but the most likely for the one on the Hatch list, was born in Lenham Heath in 1880, the elder brother of Bertie and son of Albert and Ellen. This Fred married quite young and moved away with his wife Emily. By 1911 he was 31 and working as a labourer at a sandpit in Aylesford. He – if it is the correct Fred Chapman – joined the Royal Horse Artillery.

There were yet more Chapmans in Lenham Heath during the First World War but the fourth Chapman on the Hatch list, Amos, came from Boughton Malherbe. He was 21 in 1917 and the son of another Amos who was a farm labourer at Grafty Green. Amos junior however was an assistant general carrier in 1911, and served with the Royal Navy.

The second George Coppins included on the Hatch list, who had been born in Smarden, the son of Everden and Alice Coppins, joined the 5th Buffs, having been working as a labourer. In 1917 he was 21 and serving with the Mesopotamian Expeditionary Force. He had reached the Asiatic theatre of war on 9th December 1915, perhaps – as evacuations were about to begin – going directly to Egypt rather than Gallipoli as Frank Wickens had done some three months earlier. George's connection with Lenham is not known but there were many people with the name of Coppins living here, so he might have been living with relatives and working locally.

Fred Couchman perhaps knew Mesopotamia too. He certainly knew the desert, because he later told a Lenham resident that he had been 'bitten by a camel', when he was serving in the war. He served as a mechanic in the RAF, which had been reformed from the former Royal Flying Corps on 1st April 1918. When Fred and his brother Frank, also in the RAF as a corporal mechanic, joined the service is not known, however. The RFC had had a small force in Mesopotamia from the middle of 1916 and it had greatly enlarged with time, playing a significant role in the fight against the Turks. Their service could have been elsewhere in the Middle East for the RFC/RAF had other bases.

Couchman's Garage and cars in Maidstone Road, Lenham. Either Fred or Frank Couchman is furthest from the camera. It is possible that one of the cars is Dr Temperley Grey's, who was a motor car enthusiast.

At least one of the Couchman brothers, Frank, came to Lenham from Teynham before the war. Frank was the elder brother at 24 in 1911, when he was boarding with the appealingly named Elizabeth Taylor in Chapel Villa, Lenham and working as a cycle agent. Fred who was nine years younger than Frank may or may not have joined him before the war.

George Gurr, Percy's brother, who was too young for the war and tackled farming instead

Percy Gurr, as he was known although his formal name was John Percy, was one of four brothers; three of them served in the war, Edward (Ted), Percy and William, but the fourth, George, was too young. Their parents were Joseph and Tamar Gurr, and the family had come from Uckfield in Sussex. By the time war broke out, however, they were living at East Lenham Farm where Percy was a 'cowman'. Ted who was 22 in 1917 and an assistant milkman, served in the Royal West Kent Regiment, in which Percy also served. Percy was in the 11th Battalion, which reached France in May 1916. Percy was 28 in 1917 and engaged to be married to Ethel Wilding who lived in Robertsbridge in Sussex. He had enlisted in 1915 when he was living in Chapel Farm Cottage.

Percy and Ted's brother William served in the Royal West Kent Regiment, but no more details seem to survive and there were two William Gurrs on the Regiment's strength. The Hatch list William Gurr was formally Joseph William but no Joseph William Gurrs appear on the Regimental lists, making it difficult to identify which of the Williams belonged to Lenham. One of them had served as a Territorial prewar before joining the Royal West Kent regiment and later transferred to the Buffs with whom he served first in Gallipoli and then in Egypt. However the Lenham Heath William Gurr was only eleven years old in 1911, so it seems highly unlikely that he would have joined the Territorials prewar, even if like Charles Ottaway it's conceivable he enlisted at a very early age for the war. The other William Gurr has no identifying details.

Albert Hogben was born in Lenham, the son of farm labourer Abraham and his wife Rose, and he was 21 in 1917. He too was a farm labourer and when he enlisted for the Buffs he was living in Lenham Heath. He joined the 6th Battalion the Buffs and rose to become a corporal.

Walter Holbrook was a boot repairer and harness maker, perhaps working for Alfred Palmer in The Limes. Walter was 36 when he enlisted in 1917 for

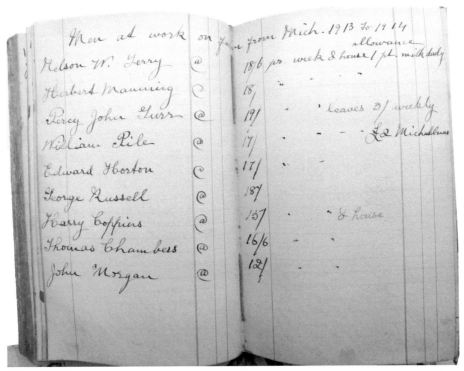

Only a year earlier Percy Gurr had been living and working on Andrew Barr's East Lenham farm, as is shown on this page from Andrew Barr's account book, here named Percy John. Also shown working there is John Morgan who served in the war.

the Royal Engineers, married and living in Violet Cottage in Lenham. Violet Cottage is thought to have been in the High Street, the present Yew Tree cottage.

Another storekeeper who saw his son leave for war was grocer and Grafty Green postmaster William Bellingham. Philip was 20 in 1917, and he served in the newly formed Labour Corps.

Frederick Pearl, from Essex by birth, was living alone in Leading Cross Green in 1911. He was a corn merchant's clerk, presumably working for L.J. Clark, and he joined the Royal Army Medical Corps as a private.

There were five men from Lenham with the surname Terry who served in the war, two of whom were named Frank. One of the two Franks worked in the draper's shop as an assistant, Frank Edward Terry. He was living in the High Street when he enlisted, the son of John and Adelaide. Frank was 23 in 1917 and served in the Rifle Brigade. His older brother Sidney had already left home by 1911; he was then aged 19 and was boarding in Herne Hill, working as a salesman in millinery. The night the census was taken, however, he had visitors from Lenham. One of Sam and Maria Clark's sons, 28-year-old Percy, a general drapery salesman, was staying there with his wife Rose and their baby son Jack. By 1917, however, Percy was away serving in the Royal West Surreys, and Sidney himself was a sergeant in the Royal Fusiliers, something that would have been inconceivable at that happy gathering six years earlier.

The second Frank Terry, Frank Henry and known as Harry, was the son of George and Jane Terry of Cherry Farm in Lenham Heath; before that the family was living at Shepheards Farm, also in Lenham Heath. Harry enlisted and became a sergeant with the 6th Battalion Buffs, which reached France in June 1915 as part of 37th Brigade, 12th Division. The division was to take part in the Battle of Loos.

William Terry was brother to Sidney and Frank Edward Terry who were living in the High Street. However at 28 in 1911, he was much older than his brothers and was already married to Nellie Westover. He was a relief signalman and served during the war in the Royal Army Medical Corps. Hubert Terry, the fourth brother, was too young to serve.

Born in Wychling, John Millgate was the son of John Crump Millgate and his wife Susanna, although John chose to serve under the name of Crump. His father John was the farmer at Brockton Farm in Charing Heath in 1891 but by 1911 he was 59, working as a farm bailiff and living in Westgate on Sea. His son John, who was twelve in 1901, could not be traced on the census taken ten years later; the probable reason is that he had emigrated to Australia. Certainly he served in the war with the Australian Light Trench Mortar Battery.

Albert Spooner and his brother Arthur were born in Egerton, but by 1911 they were living in Sandway. Arthur was then 17, and a gardener; Albert was 16 and a farm labourer. Their mother Emma was widowed and she too took in laundry for a living, as did Ellen Viner. Arthur went into the Kent Cyclists and then it seems the Royal West Kent Regiment, while Albert joined the 1st Battalion Royal East Kent Regiment. The 1st Buffs were in 6th division which was in France from 1914 onwards and took part in the Battle of Cambrai which began on 20th November 1916 and in which tanks came into their own for the first time making a material difference to the outcome.

Albert Town served in the Royal West Kent Regiment, as did Arthur (see Chapter 3) although there is no known relationship between them. Albert was the son of George Clifton and Ann Town, his housekeeper and later Mrs Clifton, and was born in Liverton Hill, where George was a farmer. Albert worked for him, taking care of the horses. In September 1914, however, he had volunteered in Canterbury, and since September 1915 he had been with the 8th Battalion East Kent Regiment, the Buffs.

By the end of 1917 the fighting in the mud and devastation of the Ypres battlefield had slowed. On the Balkan front there were some successes, but Russia, in the throes of revolution, was withdrawing from the war. British troops in Italy had participated in the last great offensive by the combined Austro-Hungarian Empire and Germany at the Piave river. On the Palestinian front Jerusalem had at last been taken, with General Allenby respectfully entering the holy city on foot. Baghdad too was now under British control. The first American troops had landed at St Nazaire but had to train and build up port defences for future arrivals, so no active part was played in the war by them until November when a small force was engaged and almost wiped out through insufficient training.

On the home front the air raids from Gotha aircraft continued over the country. Dover had 13 air raid warnings in September alone, and in December they were still taking place.

On Lenham's home front, VADs Meg Woolley, Norah Maylam, Mrs Etherington, Mrs Clark and possibly by now Meg's young sister Betty faced a new chapter at Dr Temperley Grey's VAD hospital. Representatives from the Canadian administration HQ based at Shorncliffe had paid several visits both to the newly built sanatorium on the downs at Lenham and to Stanfield House. The result was that in October 1917 the Lenham Sanatorium for the Treatment of Tubercular Canadian Soldiers was redesignated a Canadian Special Hospital with 150 beds, for all their sick and wounded, a task in which Stanfield House supported them. By December the hospital was ready for business, and two patients moved in on the 10th, closely followed by many more.

In November Mrs Etherington officially inspected the hospital on the downs, together with her husband's stand-in curate, the Reverend P.M. Taylor. Christmas was coming, and bleak though it was in many ways the hospital not only had an informal dance for the staff, but put on two concerts, one from local sources, another put on by a London concert party. As they convalesced the Canadian soldiers were frequently seen in Lenham Square and very popular with the village children – as one of Jack Hughes' children, Esme, recalled.

The food shortage increased in gravity in the latter part of 1917 and affected Lenham, as elsewhere. The Food Control Committees had been busy. It became illegal to throw rice at a wedding, for instance, and starch could no longer be used in laundry, which must have affected Ellen Viner badly. Corn could not be used to feed horses – such as were left, because many of them had already been requisitioned by the army. It was forbidden to feed stray dogs, bakers could only produce regulation bread made from barley rice, maize beans or oatmeal, although they were permitted to add potato in proportion of 1 lb to 7 lb of flour. The many other regulations included muffins disappearing from the menu and the inmates of Maidstone workhouse being presented with cornflour instead of Christmas pudding.

Food kitchens had been initiated, with Queen Mary taking her turn at the ladle on one occasion. She served one aged gentlemen his plateful with which he shuffled off without a word. When told outside who the lady with the ladle was he shuffled right back in to take off his hat to her.

Britain was united in trying to cope. One public information film endeavoured to cover the whole war effort in a cartoon of ten whole minutes. A caricatured Kaiser sharpens his knife to carve the world up, a caricatured Britannia wakes a drowsy John Bull, cartoon characters appear from all parts of the Empire, Woman Power grows from a tiny cartoon to a massive one, ship power is represented, munitions and armies. This was 1917, and Britannia is naturally seen as victorious at the film's end. A happy ending which was by no means certain on 31st December 1917.

What happened to the men from Lenham?
Philip Bellingham returned to Grafty Green where his father remained grocer and postmaster for many years.

Amos Chapman who went into the Royal Navy survived the war and returned to Boughton Malherbe.

Bertie Friend Chapman died of his wounds on 2nd July 1917. His battalion, 1st The Buffs (East Kent Regiment) was fighting at the Somme with 6th Division, during which Bertie was wounded in the wrist. The following year he was wounded again, shot in the head and leg, and this time did not recover. Among the poignant items returned to his mother were his pipe and lighter.

Fred Chapman: survived the war and returned to the Lenham area. He joined the St John Ambulance in the 1930s.

William Chapman survived the war, and his half brother Leslie, the son of the elder William Chapman's second wife Elizabeth Sage, remembers as a very young child seeing his half brother come home in uniform. William became a coachman at Egerton House and – perhaps when motor cars had entirely superseded carriages – he turned to breaking in and training horses.

George Coppins died on 22nd January 1917, and is commemorated on the Basra Memorial. There had been heavy fighting when the British and Indian forces launched a strong and eventually successful attack on the Turkish positions early in the year.

Fred and Frank Couchman returned to Lenham where they established a garage in Maidstone Road. From being a cycle agent and repairer Frank turned to motor cars. By 1938 the business is listed in *Kelly's Directory* as Frank Couchman, motor engineer, The Garage. The Couchman brothers were well known in Lenham not least because they ran the school bus and taxi service. They were also involved with the creation of the Lenham Memorial Cross in 1921. A current resident remembers Fred, who was living in Wickham House, supplying her as a child with plenty of jigsaws.

Edward Gurr (Ted): Ted Gurr was listed as officially 'missing' early in 1917; he was in fact a prisoner of war. The news of his being missing must have been an added grief to his parents as it came about the same time as his brother's death (see below). Ted survived, however, and after the war went to live in Charing.

William Gurr: survived the war and moved to West Malling.

John Percy Gurr (known as Percy): The 11th Battalion suffered heavy losses at the Somme, particularly in September where over half its strength were casualties. Percy died of wounds in January 1917. The battalion was later to make its mark at Ypres, but at the end of the war his medals were returned by the family, perhaps as a sign of the grief and bitterness it still felt. The Gurr family still lives in Lenham.

Albert Hogben: Corporal Hogben died on 30th November 1917 aged 21, and is commemorated on the Cambrai Memorial. The 6th Battalion Buffs became part of the 12th (Eastern) Division, and he was killed during the battle of Cambrai from 20th November to 30th December.

Walter Holbrook survived the war, returned to Lenham and became a postman, living in the High Street.

John Millgate died at Ypres on 8th June 1917 aged 28.

John Percy Gurr's grave at Lijssenthoek Military Cemetery in Belgium

Frederick Pearl survived the war.

Albert Spooner: Albert was killed on 22nd November 1917, and is buried at Tincourt British cemetery. The 1st Battalion Buffs were in 6th Division fighting during the Cambrai operations.

Arthur Spooner survived the war.

Frank Edward Terry returned to Lenham and worked for many years in Manktelows, the draper's shop where the current bakery stands. Ambrose J. Manktelow also served in the war (see Chapter 6) and returned to take over the shop.

Frank Henry Terry: Sergeant Frank Henry Terry (Harry) died aged 19 on 9th August 1917, and is commemorated on the Arras Memorial. In August 1917 he was with the 6th Battalion Buffs in the 12th (Eastern Division) which at that time was holding the line at Monchy-le-Preux, mounting raids and small scale attacks. He was greatly mourned, not only at home but by his comrades. His platoon lieutenant wrote to Harry's family: 'I cannot tell you how much we shall miss your boy.'

Sidney and *William Terry,* the brothers of Frank Edward Terry, also survived the war. William born in 1883 became a police constable, and died at the age of 49 of blood poisoning after helping at a post mortem, a job that ties in with his service with the Royal Army Medical Corps.

Albert Charles Town died of wounds on 10th June 1917, while his battalion was in action at the Battle of Messines, the prelude to the Third Battle of Ypres offensive.

Five

When Winter's Dead

From 'The Thrush' by Edward Thomas

The year of 1918 was to bring the Armistice, but at its beginning there seemed no end to the war in sight; much as each participant longed for peace it had to plan for war. The deadlock on the Western front continued as the Germans planned a new offensive with attacks from Arras down to St Quentin in the hope of breaking through to the Channel ports. With a supreme effort at Arras and at the 1918 battles for the Somme the Allies managed to hold the Germans off. The American forces at last entered the fight in February in the French sector and although Russia signed a peace treaty with Germany in March the situation in the summer of 1918 began to look more hopeful in France and Flanders. In Salonika the Greeks joined the Allies in an offensive bitterly fought which led to victory in

The cruiser *Vindictive* after her return from Zeebrugge. She would be used as a blocking vessel and sunk during the second operation at Ostend.

the autumn, and fighting in Mesopotamia and Palestine led to the Allies' success against the Turks, who surrendered in October, followed by the Austro Hungarian empire in early November. At sea in April an operation to block the Germans' canal submarine and shipping exit to the North Sea at Zeebrugge and later at Ostend, although only partially successful, was a great morale booster at home. The obsolete cruiser HMS *Vindictive* was badly damaged at Zeebrugge and was then sunk as a blocking vessel in the Ostend operation three weeks later. No less than 11 Victoria Crosses were awarded, eight of them for Zeebrugge, including one to the *Vindictive's* Captain Carpenter.

At home the war had taken its toll on everyday living. The food shortage grew worse and therefore the controls grew ever harsher, and the food and coal queues longer. It didn't help that the winter had been a bitterly cold one, as the men in the trenches at Ypres knew all too well. Meat grew scarce as did dairy food, and queues grew ever longer. The Gotha raids continued to wreak havoc on London and Kent, with a raid on 29th January in which 67 people were killed and 166 injured. In London the American author of the popular song 'Keep the Home Fires Burning', Lena Guilbert Ford, was killed with her son in a Gotha raid on 7th March 1918, the first US casualties to die this way, and there was heavy loss of life, particularly to children, in the East End of London.

Air raid threats were constant. Here Dover citizens are seen taking cover in the vaults of the Phoenix Brewery.

In February there were 18 casualties at Dover and several more in London killing many people. And the raids continued for some while. Lenham was in prime position to see activity for it was near to the base of 53 Wing, formed at Harrietsham in March 1918 with No 50 Squadron flying BE2cs and Sopwith Camels. The squadron had been founded at Dover in May 1916 for home defence roles; it had flights at various airfields in Kent and by October in 1918 it was using the Sopwith Camels as night fighters. From November onwards it flew SE5s and in the following month it briefly acquired a new and famous CO before it was disbanded in 1919 – Major Arthur Harris, later to be head of Bomber Command in World War 2.

Women were filling in the gaps in local services. Here a postwoman is seen outside Cygnet Cottages in Sandway.

In Lenham a Patients' Comfort Fund had been set up by the village for the sanatorium and Stanfield House, and fundraising was in full flow on the evening of 25th January when a concert was held in the Village Institute. A day later there was a stark reminder of the war when the sanatorium received a now familiar communication at 7.55 pm. 'Take Air Raid Action. Field Marshal's orders.' The next night there was also a warning and on many nights thereafter.

On recovering sufficient strength, patients were regularly transferred to Liverpool for repatriation to Canada, and in February 50 were well enough to go. Sadly not all patients survived their wounds or illnesses, and there were periodic funerals held by the Reverend Taylor, with burials in Lenham Cemetery. In March Private Johnson was interred with full military honours, including a band, as was the case with all the casualties. In April Captain the Reverend Francis Etherington returned on leave and was able to take a service himself at the hospital, but by May he had left for Egypt again and it was the Reverend Taylor who took the service when another Canadian patient died, Private Robinson. In the same month the village organised another evening concert for both hospitals which took place in the open air in front of Stanfield House. Luckily the weather was bright and hot that day!

The concert for the wounded and sick troops must have rammed home once again the numbers of Lenham men serving abroad not to mention the numbers of men still leaving. The landlord of the Red Lion, George Chambers, and

Norton Chambers, one of the three sons of George Chambers at the Red Lion pub who served in the war

his wife Mary now had three sons at war, Charles, Norton and Harry. Norton, a carpenter in the family wood business, was 28 in 1918 and he had first enlisted in the Royal East Kent Yeomanry, then transferred to the Royal Engineers. His brother Harry, who was his father's assistant in the pub, was two years younger than Norton and was serving with the Royal West Kent Regiment. Charles was the youngest of the three at 21; he joined the Royal West Surrey Regiment and later the Machine Gun Corps, Infantry 49th battalion.

The Chaney family who lived at Corks Court farm at Platt's Heath had two sons overseas. Thomas and Florence Chaney's family eventually numbered nine, not unusual in the early twentieth century. Thomas was the son of William Chaney who farmed at Upper Runham Farm, growing hops and fruit. When Thomas married Florence (another Chambers) he moved from his parents' home to Corks Court, but he continued to work on his father's farm, as his own family grew. Two of their sons fought in the war, Maurice and William. Maurice, who was a great chum of Sam Clark, served with the Royal Fusiliers and William, only 16 or 17 in

Maurice Chaney

1918, went into the Navy. Maurice was older, 19 by 1918. Their eldest brother Sidney was unable to serve in the war owing to an accident he had suffered as a child. In World War Two, however, he served in the local Civil Defence.

There was another Chaney born in Lenham in 1896 who served in the war, though not known to be any relation to the William or Thomas families. Wilfred Chaney, who had been working on his father's farm, Hill Farm in Ulcombe, before the war and living in Farleigh, joined the Army Service Corps. Later he was transferred to the 14th Battalion Royal Warwickshire Regiment.

Maurice Chaney in the Royal Fusiliers

Platt's Heath School in 1902. Maurice Chaney is in the front row, second from the left, and Sidney is in the middle of the second row.

There were more Clarks from Lenham who served in the war too, other than those whose stories have appeared in earlier chapters (the sons of Samuel and Maria Clark in Church Square, of Charles and Annie in the High Street, and of Fred and Emma Clark in Lime Kiln Cottages, and Edwin Jesse Clark). One of three others (see also Chapter 6) was Lester, the 18-year-old son of bricklayer Joshua and his wife Emma, who lived at Barefield Cottage, Lenham. There is some doubt over this identification because according to the Hatch list he served as a sergeant; this was in the 53rd (Young Soldier) Battalion, a basic training unit based at Clipstone Camp and part of the 2nd Reserve Brigade. In early 1918 it was based at Cannock Chase. However Joshua and Emma's son Lester was only 10 in 1911 and though he could have been called up in 1918 it seems unlikely he would have been promoted to sergeant and training new recruits.

There were more Coppins families too in Lenham. In earlier chapters two George Coppins have appeared, but there was another Coppins family in the parish of Lenham from which three sons enlisted, Edmund, Thomas and Samuel. They were the sons of widower George Thomas Coppins, who was a farm labourer living in Sandway at Lewsome Cottage. Edmund, the eldest at 33 in 1918, was a waggoner on a farm, and served with the Labour Corps, Samuel who was 24 in 1918 served with the Machine Gun Corps, and their brother Thomas who was a year younger served with the 7th Battalion Buffs in France.

Victor Cross at his wedding to Rose Patience Boorman in 1929

Victor Cross came from another large family with five brothers and three sisters, living in Barnfield in Charing Heath. His brother Alfred was a year older than Victor, and was 19 in 1918. He served in The Buffs, and signed up for further service in 1920. Victor, by then living in Hook Street, Lenham Heath, joined the 52nd Bedfordshire graduated training battalion in February 1918, and enlisted in June that year.

Harold Ernest Laidler had been born far away from agricultural Lenham. He was born to army parents in Bangalore, India, John (from London) and Eliza (from Whitstable) but when his father became an army pensioner they moved to Green Hill, Sandway. Harold wasted no time in following his father into the army. He enlisted on 15th August 1914, when he was eighteen, and must have had previous army training as he was in France by 23rd August. He was first with GHQ 3rd Echelon Army Service Corps and then 1st Battalion Hampshire Regiment in which he became a corporal. In 1918 however there seems to have been a major change in his service life when he transferred to the RAF.

Christopher and William Renwick were brothers and the sons of Jessie Renwick who owned Top Hill Farm in Lenham, which she farmed with her second husband James Neaves. Christopher, who was 21 in 1918, joined the Royal Sussex Regiment and William was 24. He served with the Queen's Own Royal West Kent Regiment. There was also an older brother Herbert, who continued to work on the farm.

William Henry Russell was 21 in 1918, serving first with the Buffs and then with the 2nd Dragoon Guards, the Queen's Bays, which served from 1914 onwards in France, sometimes as a mobile mounted force, but more usually as infantry as the losses to horses grew. His parents, David and Annie Russell, lived in the Red Houses on the Ashford Road in Lenham, and at the age of 15 William had been a working nurseryman. By the time he came to enlist, however, he was living in Maidstone.

Strawberry pickers at Runham Farm in 1900. Seen here are Thomas Chaney, father to Maurice, William and Sidney *(back row, fourth from the left)*; his wife Florence, holding William *(front row right)* and in the row of children in the front are Maurice Chaney *(first right)* and next to him his brother Sidney.

Herbert Smith DCM *(front row, right)*. His wife is on the left of the front row.

Herbert Smith was the son of fishmonger Tom Smith and his wife Clara who lived in the Hill Road, Lenham. Herbert was 15 in 1911, and first joined the Royal East Kent Mounted Rifles (East Kent Yeomanry); in late 1916 however he transferred to the 11th Battalion Royal West Kent Regiment. There he became a sergeant and distinguished himself in his career by winning the DCM on 31st July 1917. The Third Battle of Ypres had begun that month and the village of Hollebeke and its château had again become a hotly contested position. Herbert was wounded in the same month, probably during the attack for which he gained his DCM. The award was gazetted on 26th January 1918 'for conspicuous and gallantry and devotion to duty'. The citation ends: 'When all the other NCOs in his company had become casualties he superintended the consolidation of the captured objective. By his fine personal example he kept his men working and cheerful under heavy shelling and pouring rain.' Herbert finished the war with the 10th Battalion.

Not far away from the Smith family, George Stedman was living in Lime Kiln Cottages, when he enlisted for the Buffs. By early 1918 however he was in the 4th Battalion Royal Fusiliers, and this battalion, part of 9th Brigade, 3rd Division, was about to take part in the First Battle of the Somme.

In 1918 Court Farm in Lenham was farmed by the Todd family, headed by Thomas Renwick Todd and his wife Frances. The Todds, like the Boyds at New Shelve and the Barrs at East Lenham, had come from Scotland in the late nineteenth century because of the better prospects in the south at a time of agricultural depression. Thomas and Frances's three sons, Francis (Frank), John and Herbert all served in the war. Frank was away at the time of the 1911 census, perhaps because he was already serving in the Navy, as he was during the war. Frank became an engineer lieutenant and served with honours in the Auxiliary Patrol and Minesweeping force in 1918. He was at one point in Bombay Harbour where Sam Clark caught sight of him and recorded on 25th July 1917: 'I was on fatigue work this morning when to my surprise I saw Frank Todd. I suppose he must have a commission. I didn't ask him, but he was in Pyjamas and in officers' quarters. He told me that things were allright at home when he left.'

Herbert Todd was 24 in 1918, and John was 31. Both of them were born in Dumfriesshire. Herbert Todd became a captain in the King Edward's Lancers (King Edward's (Probyn's Horse) Own Lancers Bengal Cavalry). John became a corporal in the Royal Army Ordnance Corps. Quite a family!

Charles William Baldock was another Lenham man who was possibly spotted by a friend on military service far away. Charles was born in Otterden, then partly in the parish of Lenham, and he was living there with his wife Annie when he enlisted. His parents, William and Mary Ann, however, had then moved to High Street, Lenham, where Charles had grown up. Charles was 38 in 1918 and a gardener by trade. Charles joined the Buffs, later transferring to 2nd Battalion Royal Munster Fusiliers. In a letter home written on 20th April 1914, Lewis Hodgkin in Dalhousie India, had written, 'and I think young Baldock is in the Buffs'. It is highly unlikely that 'young Baldock' was Charles however, as he was 34 in 1914, and there were quite a few Baldocks on the Buffs' strength during the war.

Sid Friend Wheeler was the son of the first marriage of Mary Anne Gillett, who by the time of the 1911 census had married William Gillett; the family was then living in Chapel Cottages, Lenham Heath. Sid was a general labourer of 23 in 1911. He joined the Queen's Royal West Surrey Regiment and then transferred to the Labour Corps. He is remembered in Lenham as having served in the Far East which suggests he might have been with the 1st/4th or 1st/5th Territorial Battalions of the West Surrey Regiment which served in India, or the 17th or 18th Labour Battalions of the regiment. These were then transferred to the Labour Corps becoming the Eastern Command Labour Centre.

Another general labourer was Edward Vant, who was the son of Edward and Eliza. He had been born in Westwell, and by 1911, at age 22, he was working in Challock. His connection with Lenham isn't clear, but in the same year a John Vant was the farmer at Flint Barn farm in the parish. This wasn't Edward's father or his brother John, but might have been a relation for whom Edward came to work in due course. Edward Vant became a gunner first in the Royal Horse Artillery and then in the Royal Field Artillery. He reached France in September 1915, by which time he had married Maude and had two small children.

Samuel Maxwell Coleman was 28 years old in 1918 and serving as a lance corporal in the 16th County of London Battalion, Queen's Westminster Bays. Samuel had been born in East Dulwich, but by 1918 his parents, Samuel and Elizabeth Coleman, were living at the Hollies in Wychling. Samuel (senior) was a school teacher and Samuel Maxwell was their only son. In August 1918 the battalion was in the final push forward along a 90 mile line between Arras and Soissons.

When William Boorman enlisted for the RASC, he was an assistant grocer in Sandway, where his parents, farm bailiff Fred and his wife Rebecca, lived. William became a staff sergeant and served in Egypt, according to a Lenham resident – Fred Cox's nephew, the late Norbury Colbran. William was 31 in 1918, and three years earlier he had married Lily, daughter of Sam and Maria Clark and the sister of Sam junior who was serving in Mesopotamia.

Arthur Bucknell was the son of William Bucknell who owned Old Shelve Farm. Like many of the other farms around Lenham, one of the crops it grew was hops, and of course the oast houses are still standing, though no longer for the purpose they were built. Arthur became a corporal in the 10th Battalion Royal West Kent regiment.

On 7th August Lenham had a gala day. Both the hospitals and the whole of the village attended an Athletic Fete in Lenham. The highlight was the baseball match between the Lenham Canadian Athletic Association team and that of the Canadian Ordnance Corps team from Ashford. I wish I could report that Lenham won, but it lost to Ashford. The score was 5 to 4. Was Lenham downhearted? No. On 1st September it was again supporting the hospitals with a band concert for the VAD Hospital patients held in the village, and on Bonfire Night in November 'local talent' gave a concert for the patients at the hospital on the downs.

Lenham football team, Maurice Chaney is in the back row, far right

By then the war was all but over, but a new enemy struck, not just in the UK but all over Europe, claiming more victims than the war itself: the Spanish flu, as it was called. In the hospital records it is merely noted as 'Influenza', the first entry being on 20th November. By the 30th the nursing sisters were going down with it, and in December the VAD hospital and patients were struck. Some recovered and were discharged, some taken to other hospitals. At the front, many men who survived trench warfare were struck by this lethal flu and died during the winter of 1918/19.

The Armistice was signed in a railway carriage in Compiègne on the morning of the 11th, after much negotiation and based on the 14 requirements set out by the US president Woodrow Wilson at the beginning of 1918. In August the Germans had been pushed back on to the defensive. With British, Empire and French forces weary after years of war, the American forces had become a decisive factor in the closing months of the war. In the Middle East Lawrence of Arabia's irregular Arab forces had helped bring about the fall of Damascus leading to an armistice on 30th October, at sea the U-boat campaign came to an end in the same month, and in Italy the battle at the Piave had led to an armistice. The Kaiser abdicated and left for exile in the Netherlands where he lived quietly for many years dying in 1941 at the age of 82.

What happened to the men from Lenham
Baldock, Charles. Charles Baldock was killed during the Battle of St Quentin on 22nd March 1918. There were other Baldocks connected with Lenham as well as his parents, and though there's no known connection it would be good to think that the Freddie Baldock who was 33 in 1918 and had worked for many years for Andrew Barr at East Lenham farm was thinking of Charles as he helped to dig out the white memorial cross on the hillside in 1921. In 1911 a grandson named Thomas was listed on the census return of Charles's parents William and Mary Ann, so perhaps Thomas was Charles's son.

William Boorman survived the war and played an active role in Lenham life, running a grocery store in the High Street. He and Lilian (Lily) lived at 35 High Street, in one of the houses that Sam Clark had built for his children (during the winter time in order to give his staff work). William and Lily suffered a great loss when their baby son Roger died. Nevertheless William is remembered today for being 'a rare one for a bit of fun'. He delighted in giving chocolate biscuits to the children of the village and as Don Ambrose recalls, he was always 'very popular; and dressed very smartly'. He was church warden in 1928.

Arthur Bucknell: The 10th Battalion of the Royal West Kent Regiment was in France from May 1916, then went to the Italian front from November 1917. In March 1918 it returned to France and Arthur was wounded later in the year in Belgium. He survived the war, however, and returned to Lenham, taking over Tanyard Farm in the disastrous farming year of 1921 from Don Ambrose's aunt Esther who had run it during the war. Arthur's father William remained at Old Shelve and in 1921 donated the land for the Lenham memorial cross on the downs. Arthur later left Tanyard for Old Shelve Manor and Cobham farms, and his sister Dorothy ran Tanyard.

Chambers, Charles: was killed in action on 25th April 1918, aged 21. He is remembered on the Tyne Cot memorial.

Chambers, Harry: survived the war and came back to Lenham and the Red Lion to rejoin the family business.

Norton Chambers: survived the war and returned to Lenham. He lived in the Square at No.10, and from a base behind the Red Lion continued the wood delivery business and also worked as a carpenter for the Chilston estate. Norbury Colbran, Fred Cox's nephew, remembered the smell of fences soaking in creosote as he walked up Maidstone Road. Amongst many other products, Norton made sheep hurdles and pens. He also bought woodland and chopped logs for local delivery. He died in 1935 on his nephew Don Ambrose's tenth birthday. There were two other Chambers brothers, Norman who could not serve because of his extremely bad eyesight, and Reuben who had been blinded through an accident. Nevertheless he was able to teach young Don how to play crib (in Braille).

Maurice and William Chaney survived the war and returned to Lenham. Bill Chaney – 'a man of regular habits', so Don Ambrose recalls – cycled every day to his job at the Westwell lime works. He remained single and lived with his brother Sidney, with their mother Florence Chaney at Dickley Cottages, where she moved after Thomas's death. When Florence herself died, her sons moved to the Lenham almshouses. Sidney, unable to serve in the war because of his early accident, distinctively wore a white bandage round his face for the rest of his long life. Thomas eventually left Upper Runham farm for Marley Court and began his own line of work, buying the ripe fruit from farmers, organising pickers (probably mostly family) and then sending the fruit to market. Maurice took up a different line of work as a Harrietsham baker's assistant. It was Maurice's job to deliver to Lenham, Lenham Heath and Charing Heath, and he became a well known face to the whole Lenham community.

Wilfred Chaney was killed in action on 8th July 1918.

Lester Clark survived the war.

Samuel Maxwell Coleman was killed on 28th August 1918 at Fontaine les

Croisilles, between Arras and Cambrai, during the Allies' last push forward. His parents continued to live in the Lenham area.

Thomas Coppins was killed in action on 21st March 1918 at the battle of St Quentin, and is commemorated on the Poziers memorial. His brothers *Edmund and Samuel* survived the war.

Victor Cross survived the war as did his brother *Alfred*. When Victor married Rose Patience Boorman (related to William Boorman serving in the RASC) they lived in Lenham Heath, near the former Bull Inn (run by Percy Clark). Eventually Victor and Rose came to live in Liverton Street, where their daughter Valerie was born. After he left the army Victor went to work for the builder Alf Clark (not so far as is known the Alfred Clark who served in the Suffolk regiment).

Victor Cross with Alf Clark after the war

Harold Laidler survived the war as far as is known. His medal record indicates that he transferred from the 1st Hampshire Regiment to the RAF and that he became a prisoner of war. In Sam Clark's diary of his service in Mesopotamia with the Royal Engineers he refers on 3rd October 1918 to hearing of the death of H. Laidler from dysentery. There was indeed a Henry W. Laidler in the Royal

Victor Cross and (probably) Alf Clark at work

Engineers who died in Mesopotamia and is commemorated on the Basra memorial. He came from London, however, not Lenham. Nevertheless Laidler is an uncommon name, so it is a coincidence indeed that Sam heard 'of H. Laidler's death' when there was also an H. Laidler from his home village, serving in the forces in the RAF and possibly a POW.

William Renwick transferred to the 572nd Company Labour Corps later in the war and died in the Lenham VAD hospital on 25th July 1918, of wounds or sickness. He is buried in Lenham cemetery. Records vary as to whether he was in the Royal East Kent Yeomanry or the Royal West Kent Regiment or both.

His brother *Christopher Renwick* survived the war, and became a stalwart of the cricket club. He was, so one Lenham resident remembered, 'always the umpire' and sometimes 'wasn't even looking'. Even so he was clearly a popular village member. He continued to live at the top of Lenham Hill. His brother Bert continued to farm and their mother Jessie died at the age of 87 in July 1933.

William Russell was killed on 10th March 1918.

Herbert Smith, DCM, returned to Lenham, and managed Town Mill for L.J. Clark & Co. The mill is now demolished with Mill Close on its site. In Herbert's time this was all fields. He lived in 'the Shack', a bungalow type building by the side of the mill, and his lodger was a teacher at the school Miss Waters, who later became the second wife of Mr Groom, headmaster of Lenham school. It was he who suggested the idea of a memorial chalk cross on the downs. Herbert's son Ronald was 'exceedingly clever,' a resident remembers, and in the Second World War was in the RAF, and afterwards a JP.

George Stedman transferred from the Buffs to the Royal Fusiliers (City of London Regiment), and died of wounds on 30th March 1918 aged 21. He is buried in Lenham churchyard.

Herbert, John and Frank Todd all survived the war. Herbert became a postman, and his son Bill helped run the butcher's shop in the High Street next door to where the Chinese restaurant is today. John Todd (known as Jack) farmed at Court Farm until it was sold to the Boyd family after the Second World War. Frank Todd too came back to Lenham.

Edward Vant died on 28th January 1917, while serving in the 4th Division Ammunition Column of the Royal Field Artillery at the age of 27. (His age is given as 37 on the War Graves Commission and the Lenham memorial stone websites, but he was only 22 in 1911.) He is buried at Bray-sur-Somme.

Sidney Wheeler returned to Lenham and lived in Marshall Cottages in Lenham Heath. His family still lives locally. (In the Hatch list he appeared as T.F.Wheeler but there seems little doubt that it refers to Sidney.)

Six

Have many gone from here?

From 'As the Team's Head-brass' by Edward Thomas

Joy, reflection and relief were but three of the emotions that the Armistice brought, though expressed in different ways. Crowds went wild with joy in London and the US, but on the war fronts itself it differed. Three days after Sam Clark in Mesopotamia had written in his journal on 11th November that they had heard 'the Germans have surrendered unconditionally' he was recording: 'Our officers have been too mean to mark the surrender of the enemy or to give us a holiday even.' On the Italian front, the news was also taken quietly. One soldier, Norman Gladden, later wrote: 'There was a heartfelt sense of relief, too great for shouting, and a deep sadness that brought into our minds a sea of ghostly faces of dead comrades.'

This chapter is devoted to the men on the Hatch list who have left few traces behind them either in Lenham itself or in military and census records. Nearly a hundred years later, some of them can be known only by their regiments or as middle aged men living in Lenham in the decades that followed the war. Included here also are some men who were not on the Hatch list and yet had close connections with Lenham, whether living here or not when the war broke out. All these men served in equal measure with those whose stories have already been told, and all should be remembered.

In alphabetical order of surname, those on the Hatch list who have not already appeared in earlier chapters are:

James Barton was living in Judge House, Boughton Malherbe, in 1911, and was not related as far as is known to the Barton brothers, Frank, John and Percy. James was 25 in 1911 and married to Jessica, with whom he had a young daughter Daisy who was three years old. Two daughters by Jessica's earlier marriage, Elsie and Lily Clifton, also lived there. James was a farm labourer and joined the Royal Field Artillery.

Arthur Beale (who seems to have served under the name Boorman from his mother's family) joined the Royal West Kent Regiment. He was the stepson of *William Beale*, senior, and aged 17 when war broke out. Arthur survived the war and married a Miss Ransom. His stepfather, *William Beale senior,* a road foreman for the Rural District Council, was 35 when war broke out, and living at Corks Court, Platts Heath, with his wife Annie, their two sons and his stepson Arthur. One of the two sons was another *William Beale.* His father became a lance corporal serving in the Royal Engineers, and William junior who by the end of the war was 17 or 18, served in the 25th Battalion of the King's Royal Rifle Corps (the Pioneers), which ended the war in Belgium.

One completely unknown serviceman on the Hatch list was called *Black,* without a forename or regiment known. There was a Captain A. Black in the Kent Cyclists but there is no known connection with Lenham.

The Hatch list includes five men from Lenham with the surname *Bolton* who served in the war. Two of them were called *Alfred.* One of them would have been the son of Christiana Town by her first marriage to Joseph Bolton; he was 26 in 1911 and probably served with the Middlesex regiment. The family was then living in Platts Heath. The other *Alfred Bolton* cannot be traced, and his service details were unknown (save for the slight chance that he might have been the Alfred Bolton in the Middlesex Regiment). *Ernest Bolton,* Alfred's brother and four years younger, served with the Labour Corps.

Herbert Bolton, who is on the Hatch list as serving in the motor transport division of the Army Service Corps, could not be linked to Lenham, though he might be the Herbert Bolton who first joined the Royal West Kent Regiment and was then transferred to the Army Service Corps. If so, he served in France from 30th August 1915. There is also the possibility that as Herbert's second name was Alfred he was confused with the second Alfred Bolton who could not be traced.

William Bolton was the son of Thomas and Jane of Lenham and in 1911 he was living in Old Shelve Cottages with his wife Mary Jane and baby son. William, then aged 25, was working as a domestic groom, and served in the war in the motor transport division of the Army Service corps.

Private William Burchett, according to the Hatch list, served in an Australian unit. There is some doubt over which of two William Burchetts he was, but by far the most likely is that he came from Lenham Heath, the son of William and Elmer (?) Burchett, and was a waggoner on a farm in Godmersham at the time of the 1911 census, boarding with a family called Hoare. According to local information, a Burchett had gone out to Australia, and this William Burchett would have been the one remembered on the Hatch list. He served in the Australian Field Artillery, in the 108th Heavy Battery, 8th Brigade, and he was killed on 13th September 1917 during the Third Battle of Ypres near Poperinge in Belgium. He was 25 years old.

Lenham School, now demolished, where a great many of those serving in the war would have been educated. There was no secondary school in Lenham at the time.

Two other *Burchetts* served in the war, *Charles* in the Royal Engineers, possibly the Christopher Charles Burchett, who was 18 when war broke out, the son of Horace and Martha Ann Burchett. *Ernest Burchett* was possibly a gardener of 25 at Boughton Aluph in 1911, and also the son of Horace and Martha Ann; he served as a gunner in the Royal Horse Artillery, the purpose of which was to support the cavalry with mobile guns.

There were two men with Lenham connections on the Hatch list whose surname was Burgess or Burgiss, but neither can be traced with certainty. *C. Burgess* might be Charles Burgess, a boarder (in 1911) at the home of George and Hannah James in Home Farm Cottages, Sandway, where he worked as a waggoner, possibly on the Chilston Park estate. Nothing is known about *John Burgess* however, not even his regiment.

John Card was 34 when war broke out. A farm bailiff, he was living in Dickley Cottages, with his wife Annie and six year old son. He served as a sapper in the Royal Engineers, possibly in Egypt, having enlisted on 26th April 1915.

Ernest John Chesson (or Chisson as he appeared on the Hatch list) was a farm labourer, born in Lenham and living in Boughton Malherbe. In the 1891 census he appears as the five year old adopted son of the local farmer George

Clifton, and ten years later he is working for George. By 1911 however Ernest was married to Louisa, with a baby son of his own. He served as a gunner in the Royal Field Artillery and survived the war. Chesson was a familiar name locally, and in 1938 there were two farms in Lenham Heath run by Chessons, one by Hubert, and one by William, Shepheards Farm.

There are two more Clarks to mention: L.J. Clark (of the corn merchant company from which several employees had enlisted) and his wife Florence had no children at home (as of the 1911 census) and he was past the maximum age of enlistment. They lived in Yew Tree Cottage. Secondly, in addition to the Percy Clarks who appeared in Chapter 3, there was a third Percy Clark. Too young to serve, he was the son of George Clark, one of the sons of Sam and Maria, and so this Percy was related to the other two. He worked in Boorman's grocery store after the war and was involved in the local Civil Defence in World War 2.

James Clifford was a sergeant in the 1st Kent Cyclists and was the son of Harry and Lizzie. Harry was the farmer at Waterditch Farm in Warren Street. James was 23 when war broke out, and had been born in Otterden. He survived the war. His father farmed at Waterditch for many years after that and was the secretary of the Rat and Sparrow Club. (This came into its own in threshing time. The stackers had to beat the stacks to get the rats out first and set traps for the sparrows at the top. Whoever got the most received a prize.)

Maurne Clubb who served in the Royal Field Artillery cannot be identified. The 1911 census shows a family living in Ashford, headed by (indecipherable name) and his wife Ivy who were hawkers. One son Frank had been born in Lenham and there are two other sons whose names are indecipherable but it is hard to imagine that either of them could be Maurne. The youngest son Matthew was only one year old.

John Colville served as a sergeant in the RASC, but his Lenham connection cannot be traced.

Charles Cornwall, who according to the Hatch list served in the Buffs, has proved one of the most elusive men on the Hatch list to trace. He appears on the Lenham memorial stone, but even under variant spellings no trace could be found on census records connecting the name Cornwall to Lenham. As regards military records, there was a naval casualty, Charles Robert Cornall (sic), who died as a result of enemy action while serving at Chatham dockyard – perhaps on the night of 3rd September 1917 when a Gotha raid hit the base, killing 132 men. He had lived in Chatham at Lenham Villa, an odd coincidence of name. Nevertheless the most probable identification is the C. F. Cornwall of the 5th Battalion Buffs, who is not listed by the War Graves Commission as a casualty but was discharged because of sickness on 21st October 1917, after enlisting in December 1915. If he died some time after discharge it would explain the lack of information on his death. There is again, however, no known connection to Lenham.

William Coveney has proved unexpectedly difficult to trace. He was killed in action while serving with the Royal Fusiliers. Census evidence has proved inconclusive. The most likely candidate seems to be Sidney Williams (sic) Coveney, living in Maidstone; the censuses don't reveal a Lenham connection, although a George and Matilda Coveney, in their seventies and sixties, lived at Platts Heath in 1911. (There was also a William T. Coveney who was a boarder in Sandway in 1901, and had also been born in Lenham. But he does not link up to any other evidence.) Sidney Williams is the only Coveney in the War Graves Commission listings and he had served in the Royal Fusiliers, as had William Coveney according to the Hatch list. Sidney Williams Coveney was killed in action on 24th August 1914, which suggests he was in the 4th Battalion, which landed at Le Havre on 13th August 1914. He would therefore have been in the regular army or on the reserves. Coveney is a familiar name in the Lenham area. Jack Coveney lived in Lenham Heath after the war, and kept horses. He also owned the Lenham slaughterhouse, while Charles Homewood owned one in Charing. In the 1950s the two joined forces.

Albert Crouch served in the RAF and it is thought he worked for Rootes after the war.

Albert Crump served with the Royal West Kent Regiment and then with the Labour Corps. He was 36 when war broke out, living at Liverton Street and married to Kate Elizabeth with whom he had a young son, Henry Albert. Albert survived the war, despite being wounded in December 1916.

F. Davis served in the Army Service Corps, and survived the war but no more is known about him. In 1918 Lenham's stationmaster was William Davis, but it is not known if they were related.

Edwin Day became a driver for the Royal Field Artillery, but again no more is known about him, and this is also the situation with *Reginald Downs*, who was a sapper in the Royal Engineers.

In addition to the Charles Day whose story is related earlier, there was another *Charles Day* with links to Lenham. He was born here but living in Sussex. He joined the 7th Battalion Royal West Kent Regiment and was killed on 29th September 1916. He was only 18 and is commemorated on the Thiepval Memorial.

There is also little information on *Fred Drew* who served with the Royal West Kent Regiment. If he was formally Alfred not Fred, then it is possible he was the Alfred H. Drew who was first a private in the Royal West Kent Regiment and then a sergeant in the Buffs. He survived the war.

Eyles is a familiar name in the Lenham area, but there is little information available, not even his forename. However he was probably *Arthur Eyles.* He served as a farrier in the Royal Army Service Corps, which suggests this was his line of work before the war.

Harold Ellis served as a gunner in the Royal Horse Artillery. He was 21 at the beginning of the war. His father Frederick took over the licence of the Dog and Bear before the war and ran it during the war. In due course Harold took over from him, running it with his mother Ellen with the help of Mrs Todd from Court Farm. Harold ran the pub during the Second World War, during which he served with the local Civil Defence. In the First War he lost a finger.

Harold Farmer, living in The Limes, enlisted when he was 18 in 1916, and joined the motor transport unit of the Army Service Corps.

Harry Feakins, who was 27 at the beginning of the war, served with the Queen's Royal West Surrey Regiment. He was a grocer's assistant when war broke out and working away from home, lodging with a gardener called Solomon Walder.

Filmer is another familiar Kentish surname, and for no known reason the Lenham Filmers were always greeted as 'Bump'. Six of them served in the war. Twenty-year-old *Albert*, the son of Edwin and Emily living in Platts Heath, became a trooper with the Royal East Kent Mounted Rifles (Yeomanry) and then transferred to the Royal East Kent Regiment. He survived the war and returned to Lenham where he worked with his brother as a builder. *Alfred, Ernest and John Filmer* were brothers, the sons of Edward and Mary Ann, living in 1911 at Forstal Cottage, Lenham Heath. Alfred had been born at Barnfield, Charing, and was a farm labourer. He served as a stoker in the Royal Navy. John Filmer who was 12 in 1911 followed his brother's example and became a stoker in the Navy. The third brother, Ernest, who was three years older than John, carries a question mark, as there were two Ernest Filmers in Lenham. This one probably served as a gunner in the Royal Field Artillery. The second Ernest was the son of Alfred and Annie, who lived at Old Shelve Cottages. He was only 12 in 1911, and was probably the one who served in the Essex Regiment. After the war one of them became a butcher in a general store in Platts Heath, called Filmer and Thompson. George Chambers was a chum of one of the Ernests because he wrote home to his sister from the Somme: 'I ain't written to Ern Filmer yet.' All the Filmers returned safely from the war.

The sixth of the Filmers was *Bertie Filmer*, who was 20 in 1914, and the son of John and Eliza. He had been born in Lenham and the family was living in Water Street, Lenham Heath. He served with the Middlesex Regiment.

Although there were several Gillett families in the Lenham area, no information has tied in with the *E. Gillett* on the Hatch list who was a trooper with the Royal West Kent Mounted Rifles (the Yeomanry). Possibly he was F. E. Gillett who appears on their strength. Nor is it certain who *William Gillett* is. It's possible he was the William Gillett who in 1911 was boarding in Lenham with Ellen Chapman and her sons. William Gillett became a sapper in the Royal Engineers, and both he and E. Gillett survived.

Four *Hadlows* served in the war, William, Thomas, Alfred and Charles, all brothers. Their parents were William and Mary Ann, who were living in the High Street, Lenham, in 1901, but in the census of 1911 Mary Ann is alone with her sons. The eldest son was *William* who had moved to his own home in Cherry Garden, Harrietsham by 1911; he was then aged 21 and was working as a general labourer. During the war he served with the Royal Navy. *Thomas Hadlow* was next in age, at 19 in 1911, and was working as a bricklayer. He served with the Royal West Kent Regiment. Next came *Charles,* who was 16 when war broke out, and served in the motor transport unit of the Army Service Corps. The youngest was *Alfred*, who had been born in 1900, and served as a 2nd Mechanic in the RAF, formed on 1st April 1918 from the previous RFC and other units. Alfred married into the Chambers family at the Red Lion, and he and his wife lived in Lenham Heath. Their cottage is now preserved in the Kent Life Museum. All four brothers returned safely from the war.

James Hamilton who served in the Northamptonshire regiment ran the Milnes box and basket making factory, which was bought in 1946 by Reg Tolhurst, originally as a haulage business but which rapidly turned into Lenham Storage.

Edward (Ted) Harris aged 25 in 1914, served in the Labour Corps. He was the son of Thomas Harris, a fruit grower in Lenham Heath at Cherry Gardens. Ted worked for his father until he joined the forces and after his safe return.

William Hickinbotham, having served as a driver with the Royal Field Artillery, became a well known figure in Lenham after he returned from the war. He opened a grocery store in Lenham Square, now the Village Stores. Before the war he had lived in Boxley with his wife Ethel, and was 30 when war broke out. He was then an assistant at a grocery store. In 1928 he was a sidesman at St Mary's church, and Don Ambrose remembers him playing crib every Tuesday and Friday at the Working Men's Club. After the second war, his sister opened a sweetshop in Lenham.

Harry Hicks served as a rifleman in the Rifle Brigade and survived the war, but no more is known about him. *Walter Hill* is also hard to place. Walter served in the motor transport unit of the Army Service Corps, and survived the war.

William Hill (not related to Walter, as far as is known) was less fortunate. On the Hatch list he served in the 16th Manchester Regiment, but if this is correct there seems no information about him. Almost certainly, however, he was the son of William and Fanny Hill, born and living in Ashford. In 1911 William Foord Hill was 32, single and living there with his mother and sister. His father had run the Beaver Inn in Ashford. William however was an assistant draper, which does have links to Lenham as in the 1915 *Kelly's Directory* a W. F. Hill was running the draper's shop in Lenham Square where the bakery now is. It could well have been a new acquisition because he isn't so listed in the 1913 edition. It's possible he took over from John Crump. Census records in 1911 show no sign of any other candidates for a William Hill in Lenham, so it seems that William Foord was either working in Lenham by 1915 but still living in Ashford or that he had married since 1911 and moved here.

It is sad to relate William wouldn't have had long to enjoy his ownership. When conscription came in he was still of serviceable age. He served in the 12th Battalion Manchester Regiment (not the 16th as on the Hatch list) and he was killed on 25th August 1918. After the war the draper's shop was bought and run by A J. Manktelow for many years. He also served in the war (see page 104).

Church Square about 1914, with W.F. Hill's Clothing store. Its owner would shortly be serving in France.

Reginald E. Hollands served in the 10th Battalion Royal West Kent Regiment, and was probably the son of William and Florence Hollands of Lenham Heath. He was wounded late in the war but survived.

Charles Homewood served with 9th East Surrey Regiment and survived the war. There are at least two Charles Homewoods with Lenham connections. One became a male nurse at the Lenham sanatorium on the downs, where the Highbourne Park estate is now situated. Another was the Charles Homewood who owned the slaughter house at Charing and went into partnership with Jack Coveney in the 1950s. The 9th Battalion was part of 24th Division and landed in Boulogne on 1st September 1915. It fought at the Battle of Loos, and later Third Ypres.

William and *Albert Howe* both have two possible identifications and could have been brothers. The most likely for William is that he was William Frank Chapman (not Howe) who in the 1911 census is described as the son of Albert and Rebecka Howe, probably because of an earlier marriage. He was a milkman on a farm and sixteen years old in 1911, and they were living at the Woodman Arms Cottages (also known as Glovers Cottages) in Hill Road, Lenham. He served as a sergeant in the Royal West Kent Regiment. The other possibility is that he was born in Lenham but living at Chegworth Court, Hollingbourne, where he worked as a grocer. He was 25 in 1911. *Albert Howe* could also have been living in Chegworth Court, eight years younger than William, or he could have lived in the Woodman Arms Cottages and been four years younger than that Albert's brother William. He served in the Machine Gun Corps. Neither William nor Albert was related so far as is known to the George Howe in Chapter 1.

R. Killick was possibly Ronald Killick, who came from Boughton Malherbe where he was working on Clarks Farm. He served in the Buffs and survived the war.

Ernest King is another whose identity and Lenham connections are not clear. He was probably Ernest A. King of the 437th Agricultural Company Labour Corps, before which he had served in the 9th Royal West Kent Battalion. He died on 18th December 1918, aged 33, and was the son of Rose King of Parsonage Cottage, East Sutton. However, in the 1911 census there was a 25 year old Ernest King who was a boarder in Hill Cottage, Boughton Malherbe and working as a farm waggoner. As the ages fit, it's possible that he was Rose King's son.

Edward Knight chose to go into the Royal Navy. In 1911 he was 11, and living at Ivy House Farm, Liverton Street, Sandway, with his parents Edward and Jane. His record is not known. It's possible he might have been the '2nd Baker' listed on naval records as a member of a mercantile crew.

Arthur La Plain, spelled Laplain in the census record, was a sapper in the Royal Engineers, and was probably the Arthur La Plain who in 1911 was an 18 year old lithographer apprentice born in Hackney and moved to Lenham. Arthur survived the war in which he had served as a sapper with the Royal Engineers and returned to Lenham where he married and had a son Dennis. In the 1930s his wife was the church organist.

Harold Lurcock served as a gunner in the Royal Garrison Artillery and before that in the Yorkshire regiment. He was born in Lenham, but not directly related to the Lurcock family who owned the grocery and drapers shops. In 1911 he was 20 and working in St John's Wood as a quantity surveyor. He later returned to Lenham, however, and lived in Hillside, on the Faversham Road. Hillside was built, as so many other fine houses in Lenham, by Samuel Clark.

Ambrose John Manketelow, who survived the war after having been a sapper in the Royal Engineers, became a well known figure in Lenham when he took over the draper's shop that had been run by W. F. Hill at least until 1915. Ambrose lived with his wife Edith and son John in the house next door, now the estate agent Philip Jarvis. John took over his father's business when he died in 1933, and Frank Terry worked for him for many years. After he retired from the draper's shop John moved to Smarden, where the Manktelow family ran a butcher's shop. Jean Peter remembers Ambrose John as 'a little man with grey hair and a moustache'.

Robert Moxon served in the Machine Gun Corps and survived the war but there is no trace of a Lenham connection. Nor is there for *Thomas Moyes* who joined the Navy and survived the war.

C. Murton, who appears on the list but without any indication of his regiment, could not be traced, although Murtons have lived in Lenham in more recent times.

Three *Neaves* brothers served during the war, the sons of Thomas, who was a general dealer, and Rebecca. George Neaves was a farm labourer of 19 when war broke out and served in the Labour Corps. He survived the war as did his two brothers. Frank was a sapper in the Royal Engineers and was 28 in 1914. By then he was married with an eight-year-old son. Jesse Neaves was a year younger than Frank, and served with the Middlesex. He lived in Doddington on his return. George remained in Lenham and was one of the grateful patients listed in the tribute book presented to Dr Temperley Grey on his retirement.

'Land' Palmer, as he appears in the Hatch list, was a second lieutenant in the 2nd Royal Fusiliers (City of London Regiment). He was probably Rowland Stanley Palmer, the son of Alfred, the saddler in The Limes, who moved here

from Maidstone when Rowland was about two years old. The battalion landed at Gallipoli in April 1915, going to Egypt after the evacuation and ending the war in Belgium. Rowland was born in 1900, so he would have been with the battalion for the last stages of the war.

Jesse Pearson served in the Royal Army Ordnance Corps, and survived the war, returning to live in Lenham with his family. He lived in the bungalow in the High Street, and carried out his shoe repairing and sales business from the garage still by the roadside. He is remembered as having been a devout member of a religious sect.

Pocock, his initials unknown, cannot be traced. He joined the Royal Navy. *Reginald Poole* was a bombardier in the Royal Field Artillery but he too cannot be traced, although he returned to the Lenham area.

Ambrose Powell, 36 years old when war broke out, was married to Lily Ellen and working as a gardener, although some years before he had been living in police barracks. With their four young children, they lived in School Cottages, Lenham. He served in the Kings Royal Rifles. He was the son of a general dealer Thomas and his wife Rhoda and had a brother Oliver who was also living in Lenham after the war. Oliver is remembered as having sold strawberries to the coaches that stopped in Lenham Square for refreshments in the 1920s and 30s. Thomas Powell, the father, had bought oats from East Lenham Farm for many years before the First World War.

Percy T. Price who served with the Royal West Kents was 19 in 1911, and living in Sandway with his grandmother Jane Burbridge. Jane was the laundress for Sandway, as Ellen Viner was for Lenham. Percy was a farm labourer before he went to war. He returned safely.

Fred Ransley who served with the Royal Garrison Artillery was living in Boughton Malherbe in 1911, married and working as a general dealer. *R. Ransley* was probably Richard Ransley who served also with the RGA, and who was living in Liverton Street and working as a 'salesman for wild flowers'. The late Norbury Colbran remembered two brothers of this name living in Ham Lane.

Vernon Record was the son of Walter Record, who owned the post office before John Hughes bought it in 1912. Vernon served as a second lieutenant in the RAF, and on returning to Lenham worked as an accountant in London. He was not related, as far as is known, to the other Record family in Lenham into which Fred Record was born.

C. Roberts was also in the RAF, but no more is known of him. Nor is anything known of *John Roberts*, who was killed in action but cannot be positively identified. The Hatch list shows him as serving in the Royal West Kent Regiment, but there are two John Roberts on the regiment's casualty list, one from 6th battalion who died on 8th September 1917 and another, also in 6th Battalion, who died on 3rd May 1917.

The Lenham memorial website cites Lance Corporal John Sidney Roberts of the Grenadier Guards, who lived in Maidstone, but neither this one nor the other two can firmly be linked to Lenham.

George Robert Robinson was a bombardier in the Royal Horse Artillery, but again no connection with Lenham can be found, save for a 1901 census entry of the son of Alex and Rebecca. He was then living in Minster but had been born in Lenham. He was 26 when the war broke out, and survived the war.

Charles Russell was a sergeant in the 1st/10th London Regiment and survived the war. Russell is a familiar surname and without further information it is not possible to be certain who he was. It is possible that this Charles Russell was Thomas Charles Russell, who was the son of Thomas Charles Russell and aged 25 in 1901. He was living in Faversham but born in Lenham. *Frank Russell* served in the Royal West Kent regiment and was the son of William George Russell living in Vine Cottages, High Street, Lenham. In 1914 he was 36. Gardener *James Russell* was living in the Maidstone Road, the son of another James Russell who was a road foreman. James junior was 21 in 1911 and became a sergeant in the Kent Cyclists.

One Russell, *not* from Lenham, was Sidney Russell who lived in Tovil and who had served in the 7th Battalion, Royal West Kents and had been taken prisoner of war after the March offensive of 1918. By December 1918 he was already back in Maidstone, however, for he was telling his story to the *Kent Messenger*. Not all the Russells were so lucky because Don Ambrose recalls that the father of Noel Russell, who helped on Malthouse farm after the war, had died during the war. That would have been either Fred or William.

Fred Russell served with the Royal West Kent Regiment, in the 8th Battalion, and died of wounds on 6th April 1916. The battalion had been in France since August 1915 and suffered enormous losses on the first day of the Battle of Loos, when over 550 were lost to the regiment out of 800. Ninety-five of them became prisoners of war, and the rest were casualties. It isn't possible to be sure which Fred Russell it was who died in 1916, but he could have been the son of Walter and Emily, who had been living in Lenham in 1901. This Fred would have been 17 when war broke out. He also had a brother William, who would have been only 15 in 1914, and unlikely to have been the William Russell of Chapter 5.

Edwin Sidwell (Sedwill on the Hatch list) served as a farrier in the Royal Army Service Corps – and no wonder because in the Kelly's trade directory for

1915 a Henry Sidwell was a shoeing and general smith in the Lenham list of commercial businesses. Edwin survived the war.

Altogether there were 16 Smiths on the Hatch list, and it has not been possible to trace them all with any degree of certainty. *F. Bartley Smith*, who served in the Labour Corps, proved elusive. Although there was an F. Bartley aged 26 in 1914 living in Platts Heath, the Smith addition renders it doubtful. *Albert Smith* was a sapper in the Royal Engineers. He was born in 1892 and enlisted in 1915. He was then living at Holly House, Sandway, and working as a blacksmith. He survived the war.

Alfred Smith was killed in action serving with the Royal Field Artillery, according to the Hatch list, but on the Lenham memorial stone the name is given as A. Smith. He has been identified on the website for the memorial stone as an 'Albert Smith' in the Suffolk Regiment who lived in Maidstone, but this is unlikely to be the one indicated by the Hatch list. In 1911 a Lenham-born Alfred Smith was boarding with Charlie Pattenden in Grove Park, both being in the milk trade. Charlie was from East Malling. There are 70 of Alfred's name on the War Graves list who served in the RFA and it has not been possible to determine which was the one from Lenham.

There was also a *Fred Smith* on the Hatch list, who served with the Buffs and was killed in action. There were several Frederick Smiths serving with the Buffs who were killed in action, but no links to Lenham could be traced.

Berty Smith served with the 2nd The Kings Regiment and was 26 when war broke out. He was the son of George and Frances Smith, living in West Street, Lenham, with brothers George who was 21 and James. There were two *James Smiths* on the Hatch list and two living in Lenham in 1911 so again it has not been possible to be sure which is which. One James Smith was a sergeant major in the Middlesex Regiment, the other joined the Royal Navy. There was also an Edward James who lived at Tassells Farm and joined the 4th Battalion Buffs in 1915; he had either not been included on the Hatch list or had been confused with one of the other Jameses.

George Smiths are even more complicated. Living in Lenham in 1911 and of serviceable age were five young men of this name, but only three were on the Hatch list. The five were: the 20-year-old son of Caroline Smith at Woodside, who was a waggoner's mate; the 15-year-old son of William and Adelaide Smith of Lenham who was a butcher's assistant, the 15-year-old son of Thomas and Emily Smith of Liverton Street, who was a houseboy; the lodger at the home of Stephen and Edith Ifield in Liverton Street, who was 36, single and a farm waggoner; or the son of George and Frances, born in 1893, and brother to Bertie and

James. Two of the three George Smiths on the Hatch list served in the Machine Gun Corps, and the third was a driver in the Army Service Corps. All three survived the war. One is thought to have become a postman, one or perhaps two remained in agriculture as one took part in a Balance Ploughs competition in 1922, then employed by James Kendall in Sandway. The other one was in the same year in the competition for the best 12 specimens of swedes.

Walter Smith served as a lance corporal in the 2nd Battalion Royal East Kent Regiment and is another hard name to pin down. He was probably the Walter Smith who in 1900 joined the local militia, and then enlisted for the 3rd Buffs in June 1903. He was then a labourer working for a Mr Culver in the Sittingbourne area, and then might have served again in the First World War in the 2nd Buffs as a lance corporal, as on the Hatch list. However from the many Smith families living in and around Lenham before the First World War he is not identifiable.

Herbert Smith has appeared in an earlier chapter, as has Lester Edwin. The two other Smiths on the Hatch list are *John Smith*, who served with the Royal West Kents and whose only possible census identification for 1911 is Edward John Smith, then 36 years old and a farm labourer at Corks Court, Sandway, and *Robert Smith* who was a sapper in the Royal Engineers. He had been born in Lenham but in 1911, when he was 28, he was living in Yalding and working as a wheelwright. It is possible he was the son of Robert and Sarah at Platts Heath.

John Stanger appeared on the Hatch list as Stranger, but no such name could be traced in Lenham. John Stanger however was well known in Lenham after the war, although born in Maidstone. He was the son of Joseph and Alice, and after the war lived in the Maidstone Road, repairing watches and clocks. He was only fourteen when war broke out, but by the end of the war was serving in the 4th Suffolk regiment.

Thomas Swan was a driver with Motor Transport Army Service Corps. He survived the war, and returned to Lenham, living in the High Street and working at the Lenham sanatorium.

There were seven *Taylors* in the Lenham parish who served in the war. *Alfred* was a sapper in the Royal Engineers. After the war he lived in Factory Cottages, as a painter and decorator, but before the war he had been caretaker at Oxley House in Sandway while his wife was the housekeeper. He was 31 when the war began, and he died in Lenham in 1957. *Charles Taylor*, 19 in 1914, served in the Royal Fusiliers and returned safely to Lenham. He lived in one of the cottages in Maidstone Road provided by his employers, Clarks the builders. He was the son of Harry and Kate Taylor, and he was working as a stable hand in a public house – the Dog and Bear perhaps? His brother Harry junior was a

The 5th Kent Volunteer Regiment, C Company, at Penfold Hill, Leeds, Kent on 22nd April 1917.

Owing to difficulties in reading the handwriting on the rear of the photograph there may be errors in the names that follow: only the first four ranks of eight are included OCCO, G.C.Mercier; Lieutenants George Eiger and James T.Hatch, Left flank, Battalion (?) Sgt Major Harden; Right flank: C Sgt Major Tassell (?),...Dyson and Sgts Lott. ? Judd, Langley, ?. Front Rank: Pte Boucher, Pte N. Spere, Pte H. Goldsack, Pt Leicester, Pt Argent, Pt Buss, Pt Jenner, P.G. Fern, Pt A Spice, Pt Cornell, Pt Bates, Pt Knight, L/Corp Burgess, Cp Wilson, Pt Ward. Second Rank: Corp Booser, Pt Stubbs, Pt Hoad, Pt Matthews, Pt Davis, Pt Mayton, Pt Storcham, Pt A. Hogg, L/Corp Sanders, Pt Pullen, Pt Arthur, Pt Fernor, Pt Huner, Pt Cheesman, Pt Brunger, Pt J. Tassell. Third Rank: Pt Butt, Pt N. Crump, Pt G.H.Bensted, L/Corp Ivens, Pt Miller, Pt Trendell, Pt I. M. Clarke, Pt I. M. Clarke, Pt G. Clark, Pt C.M. Fern, Pt E. Spice, Corp Mummery, Pt Kenness, Pt H.J.Jarvis, Pt Cutbush. Fourth Rank: L/Corp Harrison, Pt Cook, Pt H.A.Ellis, Pt Higgins, Corp Ayling, Pt Mackelden, Pt H. Clarke, Pt H. Clarke, Pt Seal. L/Corp C. T. Elvy, Pt F.C. Ellis, Pt Bootes, unknown, Pt Allinby, Pt Tassell.

bricklayer of 22 in 1911. Their youngest brother Frederick was a greengrocer's assistant, and doesn't appear on the Hatch list.

Harry junior was three years older than his brother Charles. He was almost certainly the *Harry Taylor* on the Hatch list, who served as a trooper in the Royal West Kent Regiment. Harry Taylor was killed in action on 31st August 1916 in France while serving in the Household Cavalry and Imperial Camel Corps in the Battalion Queen's Own Royal West Kent Hussars, having earlier been in the Yeomanry.

George Taylor was yet another brother, who was 17 when war broke out, and also an assistant at a greengrocery. He became a sergeant in the King's Royal Rifles.

Ernest Taylor was brother to *Alfred* and served in the Royal West Kents. Afterwards he was known as Cockney Ernie, as he worked in London. *Frank Taylor* could not be traced, but he served in the York and Lancaster Regiment. *William Taylor* was a private in the 2nd/4th Queens Royal West Surrey Regiment. He was probably the son of the widowed Elizabeth Taylor, who was living in Chapel Villa, Maidstone Road. He was 21 in 1911, and working as a baker.

Robert Thomas served in the Royal Army Veterinary Corps, and survived the war.

Hubert William Tippen served in the Royal Army Service Corps. In 1911 when he was 15, he was a baker's errand boy, living in High Street, Lenham, with his parents William and Kate and brother *Reginald Harry Tippen*. Hubert William survived the war and eventually took over the Red Lion pub from the Chambers family. Reginald was a year younger than his brother, and served in the Norfolk Regiment. He returned to Lenham, working as a painter and decorator, but later became a tobacconist. The Tippen family ran the pub and the newsagents shop for many years.

Robert Tuck served in the Labour Corps. He was born in Folkestone, and living with his grandmother Jane Godfrey in Sandway in 1901.

Sidney Tutt served in the Kent Cyclist Battalion attached to Royal West Kent Regiment. He was the son of Thomas Tutt and 16 years old in 1911, working as a general farm labourer, and living in Liverton Street.

Roland Venner joined the RAF, and returned to Lenham to work with Arch Joy until he married and moved away. He was 22 in 1911 and had been born in Bethersden.

John Vinson became a sergeant instructor in the Machine Gun Corps and returned to Lenham, becoming cricket club secretary in due course. He does not appear in the censuses for Lenham, but in 1911 there was a 25 year old John Vinson born in Ulcombe and living in Ramsgate.

Three men with the surname *Waters* served during the war. One without a forename on the Hatch list went into the Navy and probably served on HMS *Impregnable*. She was a training ship, and received her name in January 1916, having formerly been HMS *Circe*.

Charles Waters also went into the Navy and served on HMS *Reliance* which was a repair ship. In the 1911 census he was living in Boughton Malherbe and working as a groom. *Thomas Waters* chose the army and served in the 10th Devonshire Regiment. This could be the Thomas Waters, 33 in 1911, who was married to Rosa Jane. They had four young children and were living in Frinsted. Thomas was a shepherd, perhaps on Syndane Farm.

Charles Webb, born in 1887, was a coalman living in Maidstone Road when he was called up in 1917. Although the Hatch list gives his regiment as the Northamptonshire, his records show the Labour Corps into which a labour unit from the Northamptonshire might have been incorporated as this was the year that the Corps was formed. Another *Webb, William*, joined the King's Liverpool Regiment.

Fred Weeks' service career is not known, but he was 28 in 1911, married with a young daughter and working as a rural postman.

George Weeks was killed in action after serving with the 6th Battalion the Buffs. There were two casualties of that name in the same battalion in November 1917, one born in Sittingbourne and living in Maidstone who died on the 22nd, and the other the son of George and Alice Weeks from Benenden who died on the 21st. There were several Weeks families in the Boughton Malherbe area at the time, including Amos Weeks who farmed at Elmstone. There were also two Weekses, Robert and Charles, who were grooms at Surrenden Park in Pluckley, as was Walter Bugden who appeared in an earlier chapter.

W. Weller served as a sapper in the Royal Engineers, and survived the war. He is remembered as having done painting and decoration work at Chilston Park.

Charles Wells became a corporal in the 2nd Buffs and survived the war. *C. R. Wells* served as a third mechanic rigger in the RAF, having transferred from the Royal Flying Corps. *Harry Wells* who was a 28-year-old grocer's porter and living in Ulcombe, served either in 2nd/6th Battalion Essex Regiment or the 2nd/8th – the record is not clear. Both were on home defence duties. Both Charles and Harry survived the war.

Albert and *Joseph Wicks* both served as drivers in the Royal Engineers. Joseph was born in 1888, and was a married labourer living in Mornington (or

Warrington) Cottage in Lenham. Both men survived the war.

The last name on the Hatch list, *Young*, had no initial or forename added nor any regiment or service. There were Youngs living in Sandway in 1911, but this one could not be traced. It is fitting that the Hatch list should end with an unknown soldier.

These also served

There are many men who lived close to Lenham or who had close connections to Lenham and were not on the Hatch list, and should be commemorated. This includes the men of the Volunteer 5th West Kent Regiment, which was composed of local men though not all from Lenham. Some current local residents had fathers and uncles who served in the war but who came from nearby communities that were not covered by the list, including Ivy Ambrose's father and some of his brothers, the Wardens from Payden Street. Here are more who also have links to Lenham:

Gordon Frank Mason Apps, DFC, was born in Lenham in 1899 and attended Lenham School but the family moved to Sutton Valence before the war

Gordon Apps, DFC

and he finished his education there. He was the son of a sanitary inspector, Henry, and his wife Kate. He joined the Artists' Rifles in 1917, but transferred to the RFC in August that year. After training he joined 66 Squadron in Italy, where he became a flying ace, scoring many victories and being awarded the DFC in 1918. Just before the Armistice he returned to Kent and joined 50 Squadron at Bekesbourne – the squadron shortly to be run by Major Arthur Harris.

He ended his career with the RAF in March 1919, but that wasn't the end of his flying career. His former flight commander in Italy, the famous William Barker, VC, lured him over to Canada, where he joined the newly founded Canadian Air Force. There he remained, but was tragically killed in a plane crash in 1931. His brother Jack had transferred from the Artists' Rifles to the Northumberland Fusiliers and was killed at Bourlon Wood in November 1917.

Colonel Fred Harris Peter, DSO and bar, MC, Croix de Guerre

Fred Harris Peter, the father of Bill Peter who is married to Jack Hughes' daughter Jean, had a distinguished career in the First World War with the Dragoon Guards and the Royal Fusiliers. In the regular army, he was an Old Contemptible, and saw the war through with the Dragoon Guards and then the Royal Fusiliers. He ended the war with the rank of colonel, the DSO and bar, the MC, and the French Croix de Guerre. During the two world wars he owned the Victoria Hotel in Maidstone, leaving it only to rejoin the service for the Second World War in which he was a founder of the Pioneer Corps. His son Bill served in the Second World War in the Royal Fusiliers (as had his father in the First War) and then the Corps of Military Police.

John Samuel Sage was born in Lenham, the son of John and Martha Sage, but the family moved to Wind Hill in Charing Heath, where he was living in 1911 (next door to his parents because the family had grown) when he was 15. He served with the 2nd Royal West Kent Regiment which had arrived in Basra in February 1915 as part of the Mesopotamian Expeditionary Force fighting the Turks. He died on 5th April 1916, having been wounded earlier in the year and is buried in Baghdad.

Captain Gerald Hyland was Lenham resident's Lesley Feakes' uncle, who served in both wars: in the first he was an officer cadet on the SS *Umaria* torpedoed off the Italian coast in May 1917. He was taken into captivity with the wounded captain whom he refused to leave. There were only three prisoners in total. He managed to escape however and found his way back to the UK. In the second war Gerald was the captain of the *Gairsoppa* and was on the bridge when it was sunk.

William Scott-Hope, MM

William Scott-Hope was the grandfather of a twenty-first century Lenham resident, Nick Cryer. William lived in Gillingham and had served in the Grenadier Guards since 1905. He was mobilised for the First World War as soon as it broke out, on 5th August, thus being one of the Old Contemptibles of the regular army. He fought at Mons and continued to serve in France before being wounded and returned to Blighty. He was awarded the military medal for his gallantry at Loos on 27th September 1915 at Hill 70.

Charles William Smith was born in Egerton and married Daisy Alice Wiffen after his war service, probably with the Royal West Kent Regiment and from 1914 onwards. Charles and Daisy lived in Lenham for the whole of their married life. Their daughter Beryl still lives locally.

Albert Henry Varrier MM: Brenda Chambers, whose mother came from Brabourne, had five uncles who served in the First War, two in the Royal Navy and three in the army. Lance Corporal Albert Henry, born in 1893, served in the 1st Battalion the Queen's Royal West Surrey Regiment, and died of his wounds in the 2nd Canadian General

Charles Smith

Hospital in Le Tréport on 16th April 1918. He had been seriously wounded in the chest in an action that won him his military medal. His company commander wrote to his father:

He deserved it and did simply splendidly on that day, walking about encouraging his men until finally wounded. I miss him as do all the Coy who are left, very much indeed. He was one of the best NCOs in the Coy and one of the bravest.

When Albert arrived in the hospital early on the morning that he died he asked the sister to write to his father and reassure his mother, and she duly did so. She wrote:

Perhaps it will lighten your sorrow a little to know his sufferings after reaching us were very little. He was, he said, just tired and although we knew ....that his chances of recovery were of the slightest he was planning on his return to England and seeing you all again. Up to the last he was quite himself and 'hoped he would not give us too much trouble.'

Gladys Varrier, sister of the Varrier brothers, seen here with war refugee Flossie. Flossie had been rescued from one of the German ships scuttled at Scapa Flow in 1919. Not all of them were completely submerged and Flossie was saved - probably by one of Gladys' two brothers who served in the Navy.

Five Varrier brothers served in the war, three of whom are seen in this photograph: Albert Varrier, MM *(right)*; Robert *(rear)*; and Fred *(left)*.

115

George Wise, father of the late Mrs Connie Everest and grandfather of Lenham residents Marilyn Graveson and her brother James, was a stretcher bearer in the Royal Army Medical Corps. He died at Gallipoli in 1915. Connie remembered her grandmother receiving the telegram notifying her of her uncle Jim's death in 1917 - *James Tester.* She recalled his coming home on leave suffering from trench foot and war-weary. He left a fiancée, Jenny, who shared her mother's mourning. Connie was present at the unveiling of the Cenotaph on 11th November 1920.

In a foreign field

In Lenham cemetery are the graves of the Canadian soldiers who died at the Lenham Special Canadian Hospital, all buried with full military honours. They are: 23144 *Sapper H Southerland.* Canadian RIY Troops, 1st February 1919 Age 27 Son of James and Christine Southerland; 116985 *Private A. O'Reilly.* 29th Battalion Canadian Infantry, 2nd February 1919, aged 24; 4005038 *Private A. M. Bonfonti* 47th Battalion, Canadian Infantry, 20th March 1919; 167065 *Sapper Colin Macdonald,* Canadian Engineers, 23rd March 1919, aged 35; 445061 *Private F S. Oliver MM,* 20th Battalion Canadian Infantry, 3rd April 1919, aged 20; 210285, *Private R. Don* 3rd Battalion Canadian Infantry, 8th April 1919; 3934969 *Private H. Sherk,* 2nd Canadian Mounted Rifles, 16th April 1919, aged 26; 3158874 *Private W.E. Mond,* Quebec Regiment, 30th April 1919; 13540 *Private J. Randell,* Canadian Forestry Corps, 28th April 1919; 3302193 *Driver I.G. Henderson,* Canadian Field Artillery, 3rd September 1918 aged 29; 479673 *Private A. B. Macdonald,* 72nd Battalion Canadian Infantry, 26 October 1918; *Captain H. P. Thompson,* Canadian Dental Corps, 2nd November 1918 aged 50; 907674 *Corporal C. W. Smith,* 7th Battalion, Canadian Infantry, 10th November 1918; 3081123 *Private D. Soutter,* 87th Battalion Canadian Infantry, 13th November 1918, aged 31; 527805 *Private W. Stewart,* Canadian Army Medical Corps, 24th November 1918; 623034 *Private W. J. Treacy,* Canadian Army Medical Corps, 2nd December 1918; VR/3034 *Ordinary Seaman B. O'Hara,* HMS *Vivid* Royal Naval Canadian Vol Res 18th February 1918, aged 23; 2542308 *Gunner T. Caulfield,* Canadian Field Artillery, 8th January 1919; 2157102 *Private P. Cooper,* Canadian Forestry Corps, 10th January 1919; 895373 *Private G. Coming Singer,* 50th Battalion Canadian Infantry, 14th January 1919, aged 23; 2500896 *Sapper R. I. King,* Canadian RIY Troops, 20th January 1919; 1003545 *Private J. Redbreast,* Canadian Forestry Corps, 24th August 1918, aged 28; 424096 *Private John Beattie,* 49th Canadian Infantry, 7th August 1918, aged 21; 913559 *Private J. B. Buck,* Canadian Forestry Corps, 25th July 1918; ?72354 *Private C. (?) Douglas,* Canadian Army Service

Corps, 15th July 1918; ? 5759 *Sapper T. Smeluk,* 2nd Canadian Pioneers, 27th June 1918; 2245881 *Private A. Robinson,* Canadian Forestry Corps, 4th May 1918, aged 20; R 69763 *Serjeant R. V. Powell,* 96th Canadian Infantry, 19th April 1918, aged 28 (?);   101052 *Private H. Johnson,* 49th Canadian Infantry, 23rd March 1918, aged 22; 334115 *Driver C. T. Cameron,* Canadian Field Artillery, 24th April 1918, aged 18; 430212 *Private W. Grey,* 10th (or 40th?) Canadian Infantry, 30th March 1918; 931045 *Private C. Ash,* Canadian Overseas RIY Con . .. (?) RRS, lst July 1918; 577110 *Private D. B. McDonald,* Royal Canadian Regiment, 22nd August 1918.

With them is the grave of 7564 *Staff Serjeant W. Ward* RAMC who died on 7th January 1921. The hospital had closed in May 1919, so it is not clear why they are together; perhaps it was because he was on the medical staff at the hospital.

Memorial ceremony at the Lille Gate in the Ramparts Cemetery in Ypres. Built over dugouts, it was designed by Sir Reginald Blomfield, as was the Menin Gate.

Requiem

There are two other First War servicemen who lie buried in Lenham Cemetery about whom nothing is known, *William (or Henry) Martin* and *Robert Allan*. Perhaps they had been patients in the VAD hospital. They are but two of the millions all over the world who were killed or died as a result of the war. Many remain as unknown as those who appear in the photographs below and as the unknown soldier in Westminster Abbey.

The grave of two unknown German soldiers in the Langemark German war cemetery in Belgium, where over 44,000 soldiers are buried. The acorns seen scattered around the grave are the German equivalent to our poppies.

Unknown British soldiers in Binfield, Surrey

Seven

Spring Will Come Again

From 'March' by Edward Thomas

It's easy to assume that because the fighting ended in the Armistice of 11th November 1918, the servicemen and women downed tools and were safely home for Christmas; easy also to believe, now that the church bells had rung and tears of joy and grief been shed, that all would be well in a land fit for heroes to live in. It wasn't like that of course. The men from the regular army did indeed come home from France for Christmas, their long service over. For most men of the New Armies, however, a long wait lay ahead. Christmas at home was a punctured dream and demobilisation another. They left the trenches for camps in which they had little or nothing worthwhile to do, and discontent grew over the months to near mutiny point in one camp. A system of giving preference to those whose peacetime service was deemed priority in order to get Britain moving again failed.

Over a hundred years of Barrs at East Lenham Farm. A family group, from the interwar period: Andrew Barr *(rear)* holding Robert Barr. *In front from the left:* James, Mary, Jean, who was the eldest, and Hugh

It wasn't until the spring that men really began to return to their homes and many didn't reach it until the summer. Those in theatres of war further away waited even longer. Sam Clark, suffering from recurring malarial sickness, was eventually on his way home in September 1919, recording on the 7th: 'Passed through the Dardanelles, saw 6 of the wrecks of ships off Cape Helas and the old fort much battered.' He finally reached Southampton, still ill, on 17th September, and was given ten days' sick leave.

Facing a war situation the like

of which they had never had to handle before, the authorities found that problems such as organising POW returns took a long time to resolve, with the result that some POWs had terrible experiences left to themselves to walk back to France from Germany or Austria.

Hospitals did their best to cope with the shell shocked and the disabled, but once their treatment was over the men had to face a lifetime of coping with it. Men like Fred Cox. Wilfred Owen expressed their plight in a poem, 'Disabled', in which the last verse ran:

> Tonight he noticed how the women's eyes
> Passed from him, to the strong men that were whole.
> How cold and late it is! Why don't they come
> And put him to bed? Why don't they come?

Communication was also hard. Just as they had hidden the true ghastliness of the war from their families in the letters they wrote home, most servicemen found it hard to speak of their experiences when they returned, missing the understanding comradeship of those with whom they had endured it. Many were anxious about returning, nervous of what they might find, the missing faces of those who had died during four years of war, children grown up during their absence who seemed like strangers, jobs that were no longer there for them. Adapting to family life was not easy. Much had changed since they had left. They returned to a different world where women had a different perception of what their role in life could be. Many expecting their jobs to have been kept open again for them were disappointed, many failed to get jobs at all. In Lenham this might have been less difficult, except that increasingly in agriculture steam and motor vehicles were replacing horses, meaning new skills were required. In 1921 came the great depression that lasted for two years and affected agriculture as badly as it affected the rest of the economy.

What were the health problems that beset the men who returned to Lenham? Little evidence remains, save that one man had lost a leg, another a finger, another was 'odd', and that at least some of them are known to have died young. Other families had to paper over wounds too deep to heal in order to get on with

George Checksfield on East Lenham farm

life. Tamar Gurr, mother of John Percy Gurr, who died in 1917, sent back the war service medals that had arrived after his death, and a local parish record bears a scribbled note that she had been killed in action. Tamar Gurr did not physically die until 1927, but emotionally it might have been a different matter.

The Lenham VAD hospital at Stanfield House closed on 31st December 1918, but the Canadian Special Hospital at the sanatorium remained open until late May 1919. The last patients had left on 7th May – perhaps one of them was the Canadian soldier with whom Betty Woolley fell in love and in due course married in 1921.

The influenza epidemic drew to a close, and February saw another concert given there by 'local talent'. Life was returning to some semblance of normality – in the same month no deaths were recorded but a note was made in the records that a Court of Inquiry was held over who was responsible for the wrong delivery of ten tons of cement!

An official Peace Day was celebrated on 19th July 1919, which at last marked the end of the war. People could believe now that the Armistice was not temporary but permanent. Once that was established thoughts turned to how the dead of the war should be honoured, each village deciding its own method. In 1920 Lenham decided that its memorial should be different to the more usual

The unveiling of the Lenham Cross in 1922. It is possibly John Hughes who is raising the flag.

cross in the village or at the church. The then headmaster of Lenham School Cecil Groom came up with the idea of a cross to be carved on the hillside, a permanent reminder. Two delegates set off to Shoreham to study how their cross had been carved, William Bucknell at Tanyard Farm donated the land, and the cross itself was dug out by hand by Freddie Baldock, perhaps thinking of the lost Charles. It was unveiled in 1922. At its foot was the huge memorial stone that has since been moved to St Mary's churchyard. Every year for many decades the village would hold a service at the cross on Armistice Day, walking up the hillside to remember their loss in both world wars.

The memorial stone which was originally by the cross and has now been moved to St Mary's churchyard

It was about the same time as the plans for the cross were mooted that James Hatch organised the compilation of the list that has lain buried for so many years, in order that not only the dead but those who survived should be remembered. Just over twenty years after the Great War finished, those men were facing another World War and many of them too old for active service joined the Civil Defence organisations, the Women's Royal Voluntary Service, the Auxiliary Fire Service, the Observer Corps, Special Constabulary and Air Raid Protection. Many of them also saw their own sons go off to war in the years between 1939 and 1945. New names had to be added to the memorial stone, more tears shed.

Their descendants are still very much with us in Lenham, and their help has been crucial in writing this book. The faces of many of the men who served in the First World War are unknown to us, but those of their descendants speak for them and appear in these pages. Their present service to the Lenham community is the legacy handed down by the men and women who served it a hundred years ago. It has been a privilege to write this book and to meet the families of those about whom it is written and who have helped so much in sharing memories, information and photographs. I would like to thank:

Don and Ivy Ambrose, not only for their help on the Ambrose family but for their invaluable evocation of Lenham as it was many years ago;

Don and Ivy Ambrose

Andrew and Catherine Barr for their information on over a hundred years of Barrs at East Lenham Farm;

Andrew and Catherine Barr

Robert and Sheila Boyd for their help on Boyds at New Shelve Farm also for over a century;

Robert and Sheila Boyd

Mark Browne, descendant of the Record family;

Brenda and George Chambers for their generous help on the Chambers and Varrier families and for sharing their vast store of knowledge of Lenham's past with me;

Brenda and George Chambers

123

Les Chapman, whose memories of Lenham Heath go back to the Great War itself;

Leslie Chapman

the late and much missed Norbury Colbran, nephew of Fred Cox;

Norbury Colbran

Vera Congden and Mick Gurr, descendants of the Gurr family;

Vera Congden

Jenny Conway, descendant of Edward Brown;

Valerie Cross, descendant of Victor Cross;

Valerie Cross

Nick Cryer, grandson of William Scott-Hope;

Nick Cryer

Peter Davies for his help on the Royal British Legion;

Peter Davies

Sylvia Davis, descendant of the Obbard family;

Sylvia Davis

Ian Durham, who made me aware of Gordon Apps's association with Lenham;

Michael Grey, descendant of the Grey family;

Michael Grey

Mirabelle Hatch

Mirabelle Hatch, descendant of the Chaney family;

Sarah Howell, descendant of Tom Gilbert;

Sarah Howell

Janet (née Clark) and David Humphrey, for their great help with the Clark family from Church Square;

Janet and David Humphrey

Marjorie (née Wickens) and Tony Iles, for their help with the Wickens family;

Majorie and Tony Iles

Barbara Jones, descendant of Harry Woolley;

Barbara Jones

Jean (née Hughes) and Bill Peter for their help both on the Hughes and Peter family and on Lenham village in the past;

Jean and Bill Peter

Amelia Rose, descendant of Jacob Morgan;

Amelia Rose

Ann Scotland, descendant of the Clark family, for her information and help;

Ann Scotland

John Stuart, descendant of the Clark family; Phyllis, James, Stephen and Philip Weeks who are the descendants of Lewis and George Hodgkin's sister, Kate;

Beryl Wiltshire

Beryl Wiltshire (née Wiffen), for her help on the Wiffen family and her father Charles Smith; and the many others who have supported this project.

As for the servicemen themselves, they should have the last word:

Henry Allingham, one of the last two First World War veterans to die, said: 'As to what it was like for them only those who were there can tell what really happened. Tell of the suffering and misery.'

A hundred years later, we can only try to understand what it was like. But we can remember them and thank them.

Letter from James Troup Hatch
to the trustees of the Hatch Charity explaining his reasons for compiling the list of Lenham men who served in the Great War

Calligraphy by Pauline Appleton

Grove House
Lenham Kent 7 July 1921.
To the Trustees of the
                    Hatch Charity Lenham

Gentlemen
        May the enclosed list of
names be placed in the Chest
of the Trustees that in the time
to come there may be a record
of the men of Lenham who served
in the Great War 1914 - 18
    I am responsible for the
compilation and has been corrected
by the men and their families
as the notes on the list show
        You will oblige.
                Yours Sincerely
                    James T Hatch

129

Sources

The Hatch list itself forms the index to this book, though alphabetised and amended for spellings and regimental information. It is the backbone of this book, fleshed out with the enormous help given by families and those who remember some of the men involved.

The following websites have been very helpful: www.ancestry.co.uk; www.hut-six.co.uk; www.cwgc.org (the War Graves Commission site), www.1914-1918.net; www.kentfallen.com and many others have filled in gaps in information. As this book went to press, the new Imperial War Museum website went live and promises an excellent resource for the future: www.livesofthefirstworldwar.org

Books on the First World War are numerous, and the following in particular were helpful: *British Regiments 1914-18*, Brigadier E.A.James (Naval and Military Press, 5th ed. 1998); *First World War*, Martin Gilbert (Weidenfeld & Nicolson 1995); *How we Lived Then*, Mrs C.S. Peel (Bodley Head 1929); *The Road Home* by Max Arthur (Phoenix 2009); *Battle Honours of the British and Commonwealth Armies,* Anthony Baker (Ian Allan 1986); *Gazeteer of East Kent* compiled by Hazel Basford and K.H.McIntosh, *Kelly's Directories, Memories of Kent Cinemas,* Martin Tapsell (Plateway Press 1987) and 'The Volunteer Movement in Kent 1914-18', S.V. Hurst *(Bygone Kent,* Vol 17, No.12).

The story about Lassie came from www.Dorsetsea-swgfl.org.uk; information about the Lenham sanatorium Canadian hospital in Lenham came from the online Canadian War Diary; the quotations from Norman Gladden from his memoirs *The Somme* and *Across the Piave* (published by William Kimber and Imperial War Museum respectively), the quotations from Edward Thomas from *Poems* and *Last Poems*, published by Selwyn & Blount 1917 and 1918 respectively; the quotation from John Edward Sporle is taken from his memoir in the archives of the Queen's Own Royal West Kent Museum. The quotations from servicemen's letters and journals appear by kind permission of their owners: George and Brenda Chambers, Janet Humphrey and Phyllis, James, Stephen, and Philip Weeks.

Save for the photographs of Bernard Lampard supplied by courtesy of the *Kent Messenger,* of Percy Gurr's grave by Hazel Basford and of Gordon Apps by Alex Revell, the photographs have kindly been lent by their private owners. Restoration work is by Mike Cockett.

The Hatch Charity
Founded in 1913

The trustees of the Hatch Charity are delighted that we have been able to honour the wishes of our benefactor for a permanent record of the men from Lenham who served in the Great War.

James Troup Hatch came from the Hatch family that had for many years made its living in the smelting of mainly church bells, many of which still ring out in the churches of Kent. He was, as his tombstone in the cemetery records, 'the last of his race', and formed the charity in 1913, although he lived on for another twenty years.

He required that the trust would consist of seven males who would reside in the parish of Lenham and would hold their meetings in Forge House, Lenham, at a time that suited the tenant, and he conveyed the house to the charity by deed of gift. Further requirements were that Forge House would be tenanted to the blacksmith of the parish (this was later changed to a tradesman of the parish); that from the proceeds of the rents the trustees would maintain and protect Forge House; that they would pay the vicar of Lenham five guineas a year (a guinea was the equivalent of £1.05) to preach the Christmas Day sermon; that they would pay the bellringers five guineas a year to ring the church bells on Christmas Day; that the trustees would help any parishioner who fell on hard times; and give the poor of the village a Christmas gift of five shillings (25p).

As will be seen from his letter to the trustees on page 129, eight years later he wished that the Lenham men who had served in the First World War should be remembered in future times and for that purpose he had compiled the list on which this book is based. He handed it over to the charity, where it remained in a chest of the charity's papers until it was rediscovered in 2013.

Remarkably, over the last hundred years the charity has only had five chairmen. The longest serving was William Hickenbotham who himself appears on the Hatch list and served for nearly 40 years as chair of the charity. After the war he ran the grocery shop in Lenham Square.

The charity has in consultation with the Charity Commissioners had to make changes over the years. In 2007 the decision was taken to renegotiate the trust deed and sell Forge House, using the proceeds to help the parishioners, organisations and societies of the parish; the Christmas gift to the poor has been replaced with one to some older members of the parish in recognition of the contribution they have made over the years to village life. A new amended trust deed was agreed and signed by the seven trustees and the Charity Commission, and later that year Forge House was sold.

In recent years, the charity has given grants to the Lenham Bowls Club, Lenham Football Club, and other organizations in the parish supporting the parishioners. It has also contributed to the new toilets and entrance at St Mary's Church, and supports the Lenham Community Centre, St Edmunds Centre and Lenham Heath Memorial Hall with annual grants.

The charity has another responsibility too. It continues to maintain the family grave at Lenham Cemetery in recognition of the legacy that James Troup Hatch left to Lenham. The present trustees hope he would have approved this book as a fitting tribute to the sacrifice made by the Lenham community that lived through one of the most difficult times in the village's history.

The Hatch Charity Trustees 2014

Index

What follows is the original Hatch list put into alphabetical order with spelling and names amended as necessary and with the then attributed regiments omitted. Additions to the list for the purpose of this book or added previously to the original list are shown in italics. Where two men of the same name appear and it is not possible to distinguish between them they are distinguished by number. Other people appearing in the text have not been indexed.

Record, Vernon 105
Renwick, William 86, 93
Renwick, Christopher 86, 94
Roberts, C. 105
Roberts, John 105-6
Robinson, Alfred 58, 66
Robinson, George Robert 106
Russell, Charles 106
Russell, Frank 106
Russell, Fred 106
Russell, James 106
Russell, William H. 86, 94

Sage, John Samuel 113
Sidwill, Edwin (Sedwill) 106
Smith, Albert 107
Smith, Alfred 107
Smith, Berty 107
Smith, Charles William 45, 114
Smith, Fred 107
Smith, George 59, 107
Smith, George (2) 59, 107
Smith, George (3) 59, 107
Smith, Herbert 88, 94, 108
Smith, James 107
Smith, James (2) 107
Smith, John 108
Smith, Lester Edwin 37, 44, 108
Smith, Robert 108
Smith, Walter 108
Smith, William 59, 66
Spooner, Albert 76, 79
Spooner, Arthur 76, 79
Stanger, John (Stranger) 108
Stedman, George 88, 94
Swaffer, William 16, 26
Swan, Thomas 108

Tanton, Robert 58, 66
Taylor, Alfred 108
Taylor, Charles 108
Taylor, Ernest 110
Taylor, Frank 110
Taylor, George 110
Taylor, Harry 108, 110
Taylor, William 110
Terry, Frank Edward 75, 79, 104
Terry, Frank Henry 76, 80
Terry, Sidney 75-6, 80
Terry, Stanley 58, 67
Terry, William 76, 80
Tester, James 116
Thomas, Robert 110
Tippen, H.W. 110
Tippen, R.H. 110
Todd, Frank 54, 88, 94
Todd, Herbert 88, 94
Todd, John 88-9, 94
Town, Albert 58, 76, 80
Town, Arthur 58, 67
Tuck, R. 110
Tutt, Sidney 110

Uden, John 5, 59, 66

Vant, Edward 89, 94
Varrier, Albert 114
Venner, Roland 110
Viner, Arthur 32, 44
Viner, Earle 32, 44
Vinson, John 110

Waters, ? 111
Waters, Charles 111
Waters, Thomas 111
Webb, Charles E. 111

Webb, William 111
Webster, Richard Eric Rutland 34, 44
Weeks, George 111
Weeks, Fred 111
Weller, W. 111
Wells, Charles 111
Wells, C.R. 111
Wells, Harry 111
Wheeler, S. (T.F.in records) 89, 44
Wickens, Albert 111-2
Wickens, Frank 32-4, 44, 59, 73
Wickens, George 32-3, 45, 59
Wickens, Robert 32-3, 45, 59
Wicks, Albert 11-2
Wicks, Joseph 111-2
Wiffen, Albert 34-5, 45
Wiffen, Harry 34-5, 45
Wise, George 116
Woolley, Harry 35-7,45-6
Woolley, Meg 21, 28-9, 35, 46
Woolley, Robert 36-7, 47
Woolley, Thomas 36-7, 47

Young, ? 112